HISTORY OF INDIA'S HIMALAYAN CUISINE

CLASSICAL COOKERY OF KASHMIR, LADDAKH, JAMMU, HIMACHAL, LAHAUL, SPITI, GARHWAL, KUMAON

DR ANSHUMALI PANDEY

Dedicated to the Friends of Jammu & Kashmir, Himachal Pradesh and Uttarakhand of India.

Contents

Contents

Preface

History of India's

Himalayan Cuisine

(Classical Cookery of Kashmir, Laddakh, Jammu, Himachal, Lahaul, Spiti, Garhwal, Kumaon)

Dear friends, please read this book as if it's a Novel or story book to make the most of it. Just like slow cooking, take your time; absorb the information before turning the pages.... You will enjoy the journey thus!

This Book is aimed to provide in-depth knowledge for the average enthusiast of Indian Cookery. The Author have published several other books on Indian Cuisine, however the focus of this book is on the Indian variation of the Great Himalayan Cookery. Care has been taken to weave around the "if's and why's" of the regional Himalayan cookery by the help of History, Geography, Culture and Tradition. The recipes are carefully selected from their traditional classical avatar of the local and original users. The Geographical connect of Jammu & Kashmir, Himachal, and Uttarakhand gives us a unique opportunity to learn about the simple yet unique nuances of the Himalayan cookery which is influenced by time and history yet could stand tall in their gastronomical uniqueness.

The parts of The North East of the Himalayas are dealt in my other books dedicated to Indian cookery.

Best wishes,

Dr Anshumali Pandey

Prologue

Cuisine of Jammu and Kashmir is nothing less than a treasure for the food lovers. The cuisine here is absolutely different from the cuisine of north India. In fact, every region has its own specialty. Unlike in other parts of India, the meals here are highly dominated by non- vegetarian dishes and the staple food here is rice. The variety during festivals is simply unimaginable and this variety brings a new edge to your travel in J&K during festivals. One thing you will never remember about your meal is the number of dishes you had as you will be served with endless amount of courses.

The day-to-day cuisine of Himachal Pradesh is simple and very much similar to that of other north Indian states. Rice, paddy and maize constitute the staple diet of the people here. But the preferred taste varies from region to region. Thus, while in the barren regions of Kinnaur and Lahaul-Spiti, locally-grown coarse grains like buckwheat, millet and barley are mainly used, regions with pastoral tradition use large quantities of milk and its products in their dishes.

The cuisine of Uttarakhand, to say the least, unconventional is strongly influenced by the geography of Uttarakhand. Which are the main ingredients used in the cuisine found in and around the mountains, forests and lakes of Uttarakhand with a number of vegetables, pulses and cereals availability which are rarely found in other parts of the world. Where great care is taken to include all the necessary elements to keep one well-prepared for the tough climate and trails, special attention is paid to maintaining the look and taste of the dishes as well. A balanced flavour is the key to authentic Uttarakhand cuisine that is mostly cooked over slow fire and consists of lentils. Although Kumaon and Garhwal are divided in different regions; they unite as one in its methods of cooking and the choice of ingredients.

CHAPTER ONE

Introduction to the Himalayan Cuisine

This part of Northern India comprises Jam mu, Kashmir Leh and Ladakh. It is the most enchanting state, with its' snow-capped Himalayan ranger, beautiful lakes and houseboats is often called the Switzerland in India. This area experiences extreme climate, summers are cool where as winters are cold and snowy and even frosty. Being bordered by the mighty Himalayas in the north, some of the areas in these states are covered with snow throughout the year. Northern Himalayan alpine shrub and meadows cover more than 49,400 square kilometers (19,100 sq mi) at elevations between 3,300 and 3,600 meters (10,800 and 11,800 ft) and at the base lies the Tera i- Duar savanna and grasslands. Its high snow-clad mountains, rich flora and fauna, and scenic beauty have enchanted one and all.

> "***The Himalayan population can be classified into three ethnic types, namely Aryans, Mongoloids and Negroids.*** *But the truth about its original inhabitants is still a point of debate. Some also say that people from the plains have migrated there long time back and made their settlement.*"

Himachal Pradesh is a magical place where the sun sets in paradise, literally "**snow-laden province**" is a state of India located in North India. After India became free in 1947, a number of princely hilly states were integrated into a single unit to be administered by the Government of India. Himachal Pradesh came into being as a state of the India Union on April 15, 1948, by integrating 31 big and small hill states of the region. In 1956, it was converted into a Union Territory. Subsequently, some more hill areas of the Punjab state were added to this Union Territory and it was made into a full-fledged state, the status that it continues to have now. Himachal Pradesh today is one of the most important tourist destinations in India. The high hills of Himalayas welcome the trekkers from all over the world.

The profound beauty of **Uttarakhand's** Himalaya provoked Mahatama Gandhi to call this place the "**Switzerland of India**". The Himalayan state of Uttarakhand has an uncomplicated yet mouth-watering cuisine which is similar to its people, simple yet incredible. The food is tremendously wholesome to suit the high-energy necessities of the mountainous and wintry region. The two distinct regions, Kumaon and Garhwal offer palates of flavoursome dishes that are high on nutrition as well. The cuisine of the state is meticulously chosen to not only offer delight the taste buds but also to make most of the resources available. Great care is taken to include all the necessary elements to keep one well-prepared for the tough climate and trails, special attention is paid to maintaining the look and taste of the dishes as well. A balanced flavour is the key to authentic Uttarakhand cuisine that is mostly cooked over slow fire and consists of lentils.

> "*Although Kumaon and Garhwal are divided in different regions; they unite as one in its methods of cooking and the choice of basic ingredients. There are also several dishes that two regions are common but have different names.*"

The distinctive trait of the Kumauni cuisine is the tightfisted use of especially milk and milk-based products as cows from hilly areas do not yield high-quality or amount of milk. The similarity between both of them is the liberal use of Ghee (clarified butter) and charcoal cooking. Both Garhwalis and Kumaunis are fond of lentil or pulses and "Bhaat" or rice. To combat the extreme winters and possible exhausting of food, they also use Badi (sun-dried Urad dal balls) and Mangodi (sun-dried Moong dal balls) as substitute for vegetables at times. The food habit in the state also witness variation with the changing season; where in winter Mathari and Til laddus or Madua rotis are preferred, in summers, Dubkas with Chholia rotis are relished.

Part A: JAMMU AND KASHMIR

(Kashmir Valley and Mountains, The highlands and deserts of Laddakh, Hills and plains of Jammu)

CHAPTER TWO

Geography of Jammu and Kashmir

Jammu and Kashmir lie on the northern region of India, bordered by the mighty Himalayas on the North and the states of Punjab and Himachal Pradesh in the south.

The three major regions of Jammu & Kashmir are Ladakh, Jammu and the Kashmir valley – all of which are rich in natural landscapes, religions as well as diversity in people. The state is divided into 2 main divisions (Jammu and Kashmir) and 14 smaller districts for administrative purposes. Most of Kashmir valley is covered with thickly forested mountains, lakes & waterways as well as stepped/terraced fields. Jammu region is composed of plains, mountains and the foothills.

The Himalayas divide the Kashmir valley from Ladakh while the Pir Panjal range, which encloses the valley from the west and the south, separates it from the Great Plains of northern India. Along the northeastern flank of the Valley runs the main range of the Himalayas. The Jhelum River is the only major Himalayan River which flows through the Kashmir valley. The Indus, Tawi, Ravi and Chenab are the major rivers flowing through the state.

Leh is a town in the Laddakh district/UT of the Indian state of Jammu and Kashmir (At present a Union Territory). Mountains dominate the landscape around the Leh as it is at an altitude of 3,500m. The principal access roads include the 434 km Srinagar-Leh highway which connects Leh with Srinagar and the 473 km Leh-Manali Highway which connects Manali with Leh. Both roads are open only on a seasonal basis. Although the access roads from Srinagar and Manali are often blocked by snow in winter, the local roads in the Indus Valley usually remain open due to the low level of precipitation and snowfall.

CHAPTER THREE

History of Jammu and Kashmir

Kashmir is mentioned in Puranas and Mahabharata. It is the only Indian state that has an entire Purana dedicated to it. **Rajtarangini** is an epic that depicts the king bloodline and their saga for over thousand years. Kashmir had been a center of excellence for Hinduism and Buddhism. It was also known for its geographical beauty and the beauty of its people. According to folk etymology, the name "Kashmir" means "desiccated land" (from the Sanskrit: Ka = water and shimeera = desiccate). In the Rajatarangini, a history of Kashmir written by Kalhana in the mid-12th century, it is stated that the valley of Kashmir was formerly a lake. According to Hindu mythology, the lake was drained by the great rishi or sage, Kashyapa, son of Marichi, son of Brahma, by cutting the gap in the hills at Baramulla (Varaha-mula). When Kashmir had been drained, Kashyapa asked Brahmins to settle there.

Kashmir was included in the empire of Ashoka Maurya who is credited with the foundation of the city of Srinagar around the year 250 BC. During this period Buddhism spread in Kashmir and flourished under the Kushans. The 7th Century AD witnessed the establishment of Hindu dynasty called the Karkota whose foundation stone was laid by Durlabhavardhana.

In 1339 Shams-ud-Din Shah Mir became the first Muslim ruler of Kashmir and founder of the Shah Mir dynasty. It was annexed into the Mughal Empire in 1586 by Akbar. By 1751 this state came under control of Ahmad Shah Durrani, who established the Durrani Empire and ruled till 1819 when the Sikhs under Ranjit Singh occupied the territory, who appointed Gulab Singh as the ruler. He was later succeeded by Ranbir Singh and then Finally Hari Singh in 1925. It was in the year 1949 that the state of Jammu and Kashmir came under the control of the Union of India.

"*The historical conflicts, trails and events led to the creation of different faiths and religion in the state. The Kashmir region is dominant in Muslim culture with Kashmiri pundits sparsely inhabited. The region of Leh and Ladakh is dominated by the Buddhist culture. The region of Jammu is dominated by Hindus who are known as Dogras and the Sikhs. Each of these religions is presently flourishing and presenting a showcase of their individual culture, faith and tradition.*"

Ethnicity, faith and settlement: If we could segregate the Himalayan people in terms of their ethnicity in the Himalayas, we would find that those living in the higher altitudes on the southern side and those in the northern slopes belong to the **Mongloid** ethnicity; and it is something that has remained pure owing to the reason that they have a fairly low contact with outsiders. On the other hand, the middle and lower ranges of the southern slopes are home to mix and diverse ethnic groups with **Aryan**, Negroid and Mongoloid strains. And the reason for this can be attributed to regular migrations, invasions and conquests in these regions.

However, if we try and segregate them in terms of their faith, then we conclude that the Middle Himalayan and sub-Himalayan valleys are predominantly inhabited by the Hindus. Same is the case for the region from eastern Kashmir to Nepal. Those following Islam are mostly found in the western part of Kashmir, with their culture being similar to that of Afghanis and Iranians.

The Greater Himalayan region in the north is mainly dominated by Tibetan Buddhists, with them being found from Ladakh to north-eastern India.

Lifestyle and nature: A majority of the people residing in the valleys and plateaus of the southern slopes are sedentary. The foothills and the lower hills, by virtue of their rich, fertile soils, brought down by the Himalayan rivers, are relatively densely populated, and the predominant religion is Hinduism. The Greater and Trans Himalayas are by far more severe in terrain and climate. Populations in this region are therefore very sparse and people living in small communities widely dispersed across a vast, harsh terrain. Depending on the precise location and agro-climatic conditions, they are either sedentary, subsistence farmers or nomadic tent-dwelling pastoralists.

"Due to the presence of extensive mountain ranges and harsh life each valley and each distinct community developed its own socio-cultural solutions to the challenges of life, virtually cut-off from the rest of the world, but still they follow some common cultures and traditions. One and all, the people of the Himalayas worship the mountains as their preserver and protector and life-giver. Almost all communities are strongly religious, by and large self-reliant, nature-dependent and clannish and are essentially peace-loving. Mountain women carry out all activities including farming, gathering fodder and fuel wood, etc., while men manage herds and are involved in animal husbandry and carry out trading activities."

CHAPTER FOUR

Climate & Agriculture of Jammu and Kashmir

Climate of Jammu and Kashmir:

The climatic conditions of Jammu and Kashmir vary greatly owing to its irregular topography. The temperature is greatly moderated by these mountains and the water bodies. As the altitude varies in Jammu Kashmir, all the three divisions experience a different environment. While Kashmir has a moderate climate, Ladakh is a cold desert with extreme temperatures and Jammu is a sub-tropical region with abundant sunshine and hot temperature.

Jammu is a sub-tropical region. The climate varies in different parts of the division. The southern plains experience a climate similar to Punjab. The summers are hot with extreme summer highs reaching 46°C with hot blowing wind called Loo. But nights are pleasant by cool wind called Dadu. The months of July to September receives very heavy and erratic rainfall with monthly extremes of up to 650 millimeters. Winters are cold and foggy, where temperature may dip to 30C. Parts of northern reaches experiences frosty weather and snow fall.

Kashmir has a distinctive climatic condition as it is surrounded by mountains on all sides. Summers are cool and pleasant with temperature ranging from 10C to 18C. Rainfall is less and that too in spring season. In winters (November to April) the temperature dips to -5C to -15C January is the coldest month in Kashmir which is locally known as the period of Chilla-Kalan (40 days of intense cold).

Ladakh is the coldest place of Jammu and Kashmir, comprising 1/3 area of cold dessert due to presence of barren mountains. The place has a long and severe winter with the temperature going down to – 40C. Drass in Ladakh is the coldest place. Due to heavy snowfall, Ladakh remains cut off for the major part of the year. Summers are very hot in open places, with temperature rising to 45C under direct sunlight. Ladakh is a high altitude desert as the Himalayas create a rain shadow, generally denying entry to monsoon clouds, but sometimes it rains due to local cloud formation. Leh the capital of Laddakh, has a cold desert climate with long cold winters from November to early March, with minimum temperatures well below freezing (-10C to -20C) for most of the winter. The city gets occasional snowfall during winter. The weather in the remaining months is generally fine and warm during the day. Average annual rainfall is 102 mm.

Agriculture and staple food of Jammu and Kashmir:

Jammu and Kashmir is a hill state having varied topography and great diversity in cultural, social and economic practices of its different regions. Existence of cold arid, temperate, inter-mediate and sub-tropical zones at macro and micro level provides vast agricultural and agriculture and allied sectors potential in the State upon which about 65% population depends upon, and which contribute about 27% of the total revenue. Rice, maize, wheat, pulses, fodder, oil seeds, potato and barley are the main crops of the region. Wheat is the staple food in Jammu region, while rice is for the Kashmir region.

Ladakh used to have barley as the staple food, but it is being replaced by wheat now a days. The farmers are now diversifying to cash crops such as flowers, vegetables, quality seeds, aromatic and medicinal plants and mushrooms etc. round the year. Honey-bee keeping, fodder intensification, production of quality saffron, basmati rice, rajmash, off-season vegetables, potatoes etc are also practiced in specific areas, belts and clusters depending upon their agro-climatic suitability. Apiculture and Pisciculture widely adopted by the people. The state of Jammu and Kashmir has an agrarian economy. There is a close relationship between cultivation of crops and raising of livestock. The cool climate, the alpine pastures, abundance of fodder and constantly increasing demand of milk and milk products, all favour the keeping of cattle in Jammu and Kashmir State.

Cattle, sheep, goats, horses and ponies are kept and reared in large number in Jammu and Kashmir and Leh is well known for the production of fine wool. Jammu region grows wheat in winter and paddy in summer rainy season. The areas that are not irrigated grow pulses, maize and even lentils and oil (mustard, linseed, sesame seed, toria and cottonseed) in summer. Jammu has attained self sufficiency in production of food grains, for use in its province. The Basmati rice of R.S. Pura is recognized by its long thin and aromatized flavour is famous worldwide. The Rajmah or Rajmash of Kistewar and Bhadarwah are truly a favourite of all Indians. Vegetables are grown throughout the year, except the two months of summer, of May and June. The fields remain fallow only in May and June months due to summer heat. Activity starts again in July, with the advent of rains. But the hilly areas of Jammu province have good crops of vegetables in these summer months, and hence the region is self sufficient even in vegetable production.

The Kashmir valley can grow both, wheat and paddy, but only in summer months. There is no crop in the winters. Hence the Kashmir region grows mostly paddy as the staple food. The Kashmir region is bed of India's famous Saffron, Amaranth, Cumin and varied types of fruits. Almost 27% of the total fruit like apples, pears, cherries, plums, grapes, pomegranates, mulberry, peaches, apricots, walnuts and almonds are exported comes from the valleys of Kashmir. The valley of Kashmir is also known for the cultivation of potatoes, turnips, carrots, spinach, tomatoes, cabbage, cauliflowers, radish, onions, lotus- stalk, brinjal, gourd and bitter gourd etc.

CHAPTER FIVE

Important features of the J&K Cuisine:

Kashmiri cuisine that evolved in the Valley several centuries ago has retained a distinct personality of its own. The food is a blend or a cultural mix of Indian, Iranian and Afghani cuisine. There were two great schools of culinary craftsmanship in Kashmir, namely those of Kashmiri Pandits and Kashmiri Muslims. The basic difference between the two schools was the abundant use of heeng (asafoetida) and curd among the Hindus and the open-handed use of onions and garlic's among the Muslims. Although nowadays, Pundits have also begun using garlic and onion with discretion in their cooking style.

Kashmiri food is mild in taste and rich in flavour with the high use of hot spices like cumin, cardamom, fennel, ginger, cinnamon, cloves, saffron and ratanjoth. Mustard oil is used as the cooking medium. Asafoetida, better known as heeng, is used as a tempering in most of the preparations. The main spices used for flavouring most of the dishes are saunth or dried ginger and saunf powder. The Kashmiris often cook their food by heating it on two sides, from both top and bottom for that distinctive taste. The charcoal fire was their solution in the earlier days but oven serves as a good substitute these days. The food is characterized by thick gravies using liberal quantities of yoghurt, spices and dried fruits, and is usually cooked in ghee (clarified butter) or mustard oil. Saffron, the most expensive spice in the world, is grown locally. It is used extensively to flavour the pulaos (rice dish) and sweets.

> "*The professional cooks are known as 'Wazas'. These people claim to be the descendants of the master chefs who migrated from Samarkand and parts of Central Asia at the beginning of the*

fifteenth century. Kashmiri food is characterized by its vast array of dishes cooked over a long period of time in exotic spices. The seasons and availability of fresh produce dictates the ingredients, some of which are dried and used in the winter months."

The traditional Kashmiri Muslim banquet known as Wazwan, which was perhaps the most unique and elaborate royal spread of meat and delicacies and which is prepared in open air kitchens known as vurabal.

There is another aspect to the food habits of the Kashmiri Hindus referred to as pandits. The Kashmiri pundits though Brahmans have been meat eaters since the Vedic times, more so because the snowbound areas of the valley make it very difficult to cultivate the food. They rarely slaughter household animals but depend for their meat upon Gujars (Nomadic Muslim and Hindu herdsmen). Pandits eat goat and that too a young one. The meat is generally chosen from the legs, neck, breast, ribs and shoulders and cut into large pieces. No vegetarian or non-vegetarian dish, except certain kababs, is cooked without curd. Beef, pork, chicken are prohibited for them. The two most important saints of Kashmir, Lalleshwari and Sheikh Noor-ud-din Wali were vegetarians for spiritual reasons. Nevertheless, meat is often cooked in many Kashmiri Pandit festivals.

The Ladakhis eat rice, wheat, millet, locally produced vegetables and fruits, goat meat and dairy products made from yak milk.

CHAPTER SIX

Cooking styles and Eating habits in the J&K Region

Rice is the most common staple food of the people of Kashmir. One of their favourite dish is Hak or Karam sag. All their meals will be accompanied with lot of vegetables. Kashmiri Pulao is very famous worldwide and is a common dish among them. Most of the Kashmiris abstain themselves from intoxicating drinks but one of the most liked traditional drink of the Kashmiris is the green tea with spices and almond known as *Kehwah*. This is consumed at regular intervals especially in winter. Some of the common ingredients of the Kashmiri cooking are spices, curd and condiments. The Kashmiris have a liking for sweet delicacy known as *Phirni* which is made of sooji, milk and sugar. Amongst Kashmiri beverages, "*Kehwah*" and "*Noon Chai*" or "*Sheer Chai*" (Chai meaning tea) is significant. The pundit communities of Kashmir never use onion and garlic in their cooking and the Muslims abstain from asafetida. Mutton takes the lead on the table and it appears in some form at every meal. A lot of meat dishes are prepared to keep warm when temperatures dip. It is usually marinated in curd or saffron milk for hours, sometimes even for two days. The preparation is quite similar to Wazwan meats but tastes and textures vary. The classic *Naine Rogan Josh* has thinner consistency and it has the essence and flavour of Kashmiri red chillies and asafetida. The other dish that comes your way shall be *Nokur Yakhni*; chicken cooked in yogurt, served with a warm, freshly baked sweet bread (*Khameeri roti*). The curries are very light and make use of yogurt to form the base and add depth to the dish. Rohu and Trout are the main varieties of fish found here. Rohu is served grilled or pan fried and trout is usually curried. Among Kashmiris there is consistent awareness of the inevitability of winter. Each vegetable will be cut and dried and kept. Also they will keep dried fish (H*ogaad*) for use in winter.

Most curries pair well with unadorned rice which is a staple but the variety from Kashmir is starchier. It features in a stunning range of pulaos inspired by the Mughlai or Awadhi Dum Biryanis. The *Naine Monge Khescher* is as delicious as it is visually impressive. Mutton and whole green lentils are cooked in mustard oil and finished on dum with Basmati rice. In the Kashmir valley, where nature shows off her bounty, there is something remarkable about the freshness of vegetables like turnips, radish, lotus stems and haak leaves that cannot be compared to those from the plains. Crisp slices of batter- coated and fried green apple called *Choonth Pakori* dipped in *akhrot pudine ki chutney*. Kashmiri version of Dum Aloo, called *Dum Aluv* is the specialty, where small poked potatoes are cooked in thin red gravy. The most critical character is the use of spices. Kashmiri cuisine is as rich in spice as it is in tradition. Fennel seed powder, cardamom, star anise, dry ginger powder, kewra - all the warm and comforting flavours come together as a kind of a perfume. Saffron or Zafraan is used in almost all dishes for its colour and flavour. Almost all meal ends with a sweet note of *Kesari Kheer* and *Shufta*, a dessert that has become a rare exception. It is an assortment of nuts simmered in saffron honey and is traditionally prepared to celebrate festivity. *Modhur Pulav* is the name given to sweetened Kashmiri rice prepared using cinnamon, a little saffron, milk, ghee, sugar, cashew nuts, almonds, green cardamom among several other ingredients.

'*Ver*' is a spice mixture used in foods to give them a Kashmiri flavour. But the recipe of 'Ver' is kept as a family secret. It contain garlic and praan for Muslims, asafoetida and fenugreek for Hindus as well as lots of freshly ground red chillies, cumin, coriander, dried ginger, cloves, cardamom and turmeric. All spices are ground, and then made into a patty with the help of some mustard oil. A hole is made in the patty and left to dry on wooden planks on shade.

A Kashmiri breakfast would never be complete without breads, that too the baker's breads. The bakery in Kashmir is known as "*Kandur*" (pronounced as kaan-duur). They produce *Bagirkhani* (Baqaurkhan), *sheermal, Kulchaa, girda or lavasa* or just czot (pronounced as 'chot') is a flatbread similar to the roti we may get in plains in India but is prepared using maida (refined flour). These are everyday bread *Tilwor or Chochwor* as it is commonly known in the valley is similar to bagel bread. Katlam is my all time favorite bread. It is similar to what we call 'Khari' biscuits. So *Katlam* has that multi layered personality and all the layers are crunchy as your teeth go on biting the layers. *Krippe or Krip* is flaky small bread similar to *Sheermal. Roth* is a bulky bread laden with dry fruits and coconut with a sweet tinge. *Gyevchot* which literally translates as the ghee roti is obviously made using ghee (clarified butter). It has a fluffy, soft texture with surface baked to golden hue. Sheermal is sweet bread prepared using refined flour, milk, saffron and dates and has its own flavor. It's like a delicious biscuit, crisp, crumbly and flavorful.

Czochworu is the desi donut which is a small, soft round bread of about three inches diameter and six inches circumference, with a soft upper half sprinkled with til (sesame seeds) or Khaskhash (poppy seeds) and the lower crust is crispy.

Unlike Kashmir, the people of Ladakh prefer to eat boiled or steamed food which is highly nutritious and delicious as well and fresh vegetables are used to enhance its taste and nutrients. The staple food of ladakhi people are *Sku, Pava, Khambir and thukpa.* Barleyor rice fermented liquor *Chhang* is one of the favourite drink of all occasions. Breads or *Tagi or Skurchuk* made with wheat flour is eaten throughout Laddakh. *Tagi Buskhuruk* (Puffed unleavened bread), *Tagi Thalkhuruk* (Bread uncovered and baked in ashes), and *Tagi Mer-Khour (made with egg and butter)* are some of the specialty.

The cooking styles of the people of Jammu are not much indigenous, but have influences of Punjabi and Himachali cuisine. Wheat, maize and Pearl millet bajra are staple food besides rice, cereals and a tangier preparation made out of mango or tamarind popularly known as "*Maani*". The whole dish is called *Dal puth maani* and is savoured as a combination. Jammu's *Rajma-chawal* (red beans and rice) are world famous. *Madra* is a traditional spicy yogurt-based recipe. It can be cooked with chana, rajma, urad dal or raungi. *Mitha madra* is a favourite and is cooked from milk, dry fruits, and semolina. Preparations of *Rajmash* (a special variety of red kidney beans); *Auria* a dish of curd fermented by rye; *Ambal* made from pumpkin, jaggery and tamarind are favorites, especially during ceremonial cooking. *Pattode* are made from leaves of arbi (colocasia) or kachalu (taro). *Kulath ki khatti dal* goes well with rice. During festivals, Dogra people in Jammu do not fry *puris* or *bhaturas.* They indulge in *Babbroos,* which are made from wheat (and not maida) and fried in mustard oil. Babbru is served with *dahi-wale chatpate alu,* maani/kheer/curd. Dogra community cooks chana dal by adding saunf (fennel seeds) to it. Expert cooks are called 'Siyan', and community meals are called 'Dhaam' and are served on large lotus leaves, or stitched leaves (pattals) and cups (doona)

Non-vegetarian food was limited to Rajputs and Vaish (Mahajans). '*Khatta maans*" is mutton cooked with sour pomegranate seeds (anardana) or lime juice and flavoured with fumes of a burning charcoal soaked in mustard oil. *Keur* is one of the well known foods of Dogras. It is prepared by flour and butter and served with sugar and curd. *Kalaari* is a favourite food of Dogras in the rainy season. It is prepared by flour mix, cottage cheese and milk cream (malai) with water with help of a small cup shaped pot. Kalari is served with milk. The common breads that the people eat are Roti, Naan, kulcha, paratha, Poori, Missi roti etc.

Kheer is a dish prepared from milk by adding some rice and dry fruit in it. It is served at all the special occasions and festivals. Another popular exotic dish is "*guchiyyan*" (dried black morel), usually added as an ingredient in pulao. As it grows naturally in forests and cannot be cultivated, it is a priced commodity and makes an excelled dish with mountain potatoes (pahadi aloo). Saffron or kesar is extensively used to flavour sweet dishes and for its anti-oxidant benefits.

CHAPTER SEVEN

Cooking equipments and utensils used in J&K Cookery

- Aala Glass- traditionally carved glass which is used to serve water or any other beverage
- Athataech- Cloth for wiping hands etc.
- Bothlai and Chhegla- Pots for cooking rice etc.
- Chalan and Raemb- Broad spatulas.
- Chhan - Colander or strainer.
- Chhonp - Churning stick.
- Chonchi and Krechh- Ladles.
- Chumta and Sanaes- Tongs for holding hot things and lifting hot pots.
- Dakna- Lids.
- Damchula- Iron charcoal stove.
- Dan: On normal days the cooking in both Hindu and Muslim homes is mostly done on a dan, which is an oblong clay oven about 3 ft by 2 ft in length and a foot and a half in height. It has a floor-level hole, through which firewood is fed, and has usually three holes on the top on which food in different pots is heated or cooked.
- Degh- It is again a large cooking pot similar to sagla.
- Dul and Kond - Metallic and deep wash basins.
- Goshpar – Kaen: These are a flat coarse stone and a wooden mallet made of walnut wood which are used for pounding meat to a fine texture, generally used for making goshtabas and rishtas. The wooden mallet is made up of walnut wood so that it does not splinter when it hits the

stone.

- Hahkol- Clay charcoal stove.
- Kada- metal utensil which is mostly used to cook vegetables during the feast. Dogri name for Kadai
- Kafgir- Perforated ladle.
- Khalur – Dula: This is a stone mortar with a wooden pestle used for grinding chutneys and pastes.
- Kray - Cauldron.
- Krech: These are different kinds of wooden spoons and ladles used for turning the food in clay pots so that the base of the pot does not get scraped.
- Krochh - Fire spoon.
- Kunni- Clay pot used for cooking by the Dogris
- Leji / Degul / Digcha: Among Kashmiri pandits, most vegetarian and non- vegetarian dishes are cooked in pots made of baked clay. The pot is called a deg, a degul, or a leji according to its size and shape. Pots used in Kashmir are round-bottomed, which makes stirring and turning of the contents easy while cooking and also while mixing spices and condiments.
- Masala Vatur - Box for keeping spices.
- Mujikond- Grater.
- Peedi- It is a traditional small stool.
- Sagla- Sagla is a metal utensil, a big cooking pot used to prepare meal in a traditional way. It is used in community kitchens and in few households too during family gatherings for the purpose of cooking rice.
- Samovar: This is a jug-shaped metallic pitcher used for brewing tea such as Kehwa and Sheer chai. It has a long tube inside that is filled with charcoal, which keeps the tea in the pot brewing.
- Sikh- Skewer.
- Taev- Iron griddle.
- Taintha- Spatula
- Tarambadi- bowl used for serving rice or other food items.
- Tarami: These are large brass plates used for serving food. A tarami could be shared between four people in the event of feasts.
- Tasht – Naar: These are a portable hand washbasin and a pitcher that are passed around to wash hands during big banquets.
- Tilavar and Krond- Edible oil pot and its ladle.
- Voakhul and Kajivadh- Stone mortar and pestle.

CHAPTER EIGHT

Special J&K dishes from festive occasions

1. **Aab Gosht**: It is a mutton dish made using milk and several spices including cardamom and black pepper.
2. **Ambal**: Pumpkin cooked in tangy sweet and sour taste by using tamarind or mango powder ot pomegranate seed along with jaggary.
3. **Auria**: It is prepared by grinding sarson (mustard) seeds or rai into a fine powder and mixed with yoghurt and turmeric. It is then churned for some time and kept aside for fermentation. The slices of boiled and peeled potatoes or pumpkin are added to it. It is a pungent and digestive dish taken mostly with cooked rice.
4. **Baqer Khani**: This dish is a kind of Kashmiri puff pastry. It is a type of soft naan sprinkled with sesame seeds.
5. **Bazbatta**: Kashmiri vegetable pulao.
6. **Butter Tea**: It is prepared by adding butter and salt to tea, sometimes pieces of yak meat are also added to it.
7. **Chaang**: Tibetan alcoholic beverage made either by barley, rice or millet.
8. **Chuste**: Spicy dry curry of goats' intestine
9. **Dhaniwal Korma**: Mutton cooked same as yakhni with spices and onion puree, topped with lots of coriander leaves.
10. **Dum Olav**: It is cooked with yoghurt, ginger powder, fennel and other hot spices to give it a unique flavour and aroma.
11. **Falooda**: It is made with milk, vermicelli, tapioca pearls and basil seeds. These seeds give it the unique flavor and texture. The flavor of the drink depends upon the syrup that is used.
12. **Gard munj**: Fish cooked with vegetables

13. **Goshtaba**: A traditional delicacy of Kashmir, Goshtaba is hand pounded mutton balls cooked in flavorful yogurt gravy and spices.
14. **Gular kebab**: Minced meat kebabs with orange filling round ball like shape
15. **Gulra**: It a sweet preparation made of rice flour, Ghee and dry fruits
16. **Haakh**: It is made of a type of green leafy vegetable, resembling turnip leaf, but has mild taste.
17. **Harissa**: It is mutton cooked to a smooth paste along with onions and vegetables. A traditional breakfast item of Kashmiris.
18. **Kadam haak**: This is a leafy vegetable with a bulbous root. While haak leaves are cooked whole, Karam Haak leaves are cut. Other ingredients and method of preparation is same as for Haak, however the bulbous root should be shallow- fried in oil with salt and red chili powder and added to the saag.
19. **Kahwa**: A type of herbal tea which is prepared with special tea leaves and saffron. It is often known as Kashmiri Green Tea, despite the fact that it is actually orange in colour. It is rich in antioxidants.
20. **Khambir**: It is a pan-shaped local bread with a thick crust made from local whole wheat and it is served with butter tea which is prepared by adding salt and butter to tea.
21. **Khamira, Pathoru and Thothru**: Wheat flour is kneaded and leavened with yeast (khamir) and then baked on tawa. Khamira is taken with ghee or butter. Pathorus have poopy seeds, coriander seeds and peeled almonds. Thothrus are globular in shape and smaller in size, preparation is same.
22. **Khatta Meat**: Mutton cooked in tangy flavor achieved either by adding anardana (pomegranate seeds) or amchur (dry mango) powder.
23. **Khurbani ka metha**: Dried apricots are soaked in water and simmered in sugar syrup and mildly flavored with saffron.
24. **Kiyur**: It is made of loosely kneaded leavened wheat flour (only maida). It is spread over the Tawa so that it assumes a jelly like form of bread. It is taken with sugar and yoghurt.
25. **Kulcha**: Kind of a bread prepared with Maida and wheat- flour, the Kashmiri have it with morning tea. Dogris take this in all meals,
26. **Lavash**: It is cream colored unleavened Armenian bread. It is mostly topped with sesame seeds or poppy seeds. This bread has a very unique taste as it is baked in a tandoor.

27. **Lyde**: Lyde is a famous Kashmiri dessert prepared by thoroughly frying whole wheat flour.
28. **Lyodur Tschaman**: It is cottage cheese cooked in creamy turmeric based gravy.
29. **Marzwangan korma**: Chicken legs/thighs cooked in a spicy browned onion gravy.
30. **Matschgand**: It is actually a dish of minced meatballs which is cooked in spicy red gravy.
31. **Mechama**: It is a dessert in which rice is cooked with sugar syrup and milk is added at the later stage and flavoured with saffron and kewra with lots of nuts and raisins.
32. **Mehri**: Cooked rice is prepared with churned yoghurt having little turmeric and bay leaf (tejpattar) and rai (mustard seeds).
33. **Methi korma**: Mutton flavoured with a spice mixture containing dried fenugreek.
34. **Modur Pulav**: It is the name given to sweetened Kashmiri rice prepared using cinnamon, a little guchhi, saffron, milk, ghee,sugar, cashew nuts, almonds, green cardamom among several other ingredients. This dish is sweet, flavoured and healthy with saffron as the main spice which gives it beautiful colour and taste.
35. **Momos**: A Tibetan delicacy, Small and spicy momos are dumplings stuffed with minced meat, vegetables or cheese. Usually served with spicy chilli sauce.
36. **Muji Gaad**: It is a dish made up of fish prepared generally with radish or nadur. This dish is an amalgamation of vegetarian and non-vegetarian items as the taste of fish and lotus stem blend together to give it a unique taste while hot spices and herbs add to it‘s unique yet amazing flavour and aroma.
37. **Nadur Churma**: is one such delicacy involving the lotus stem. These fried lotus stems give the classic French fries a run for their money. Being rich in protein these are the most favorite past time snacks of the Kashmiri.
38. **Paba**: It is made using peas and wheat. The dough is made using roasted flours of wheat, barley, buckwheat, peas and Ladakhi black beans, which makes it edible.
39. **Paneer Chaman**: Cottage cheese or paneer cooked in milk until soft and tender
40. **Pao Gogji**: Waters of turnips cooked in dry spices.

41. **Phirni**: It is made of rice, milk, saffron, cardamom etc. Dry fruits and rose essence are also added to give it special flavor. The dessert gets its real flavor or taste with the delicacy with which the rice is ground. They are served in traditional earthen bowls called 'shikoras'.
42. **Quabargah**: Ribs of young lamb or goat is cooked in a special blend of milk and spices, and then fried in ghee.
43. **Rajmaa Gogji**: Rajmash cooked with turnip.
44. **Rista**: Hand-pounded lamb in a red, red chilli-saffron- fennel spice gravy coloured with ratanjoth, popular amongst Kashmiris.
45. **Rogan Josh**: An aromatic lamb dish is one of the signature recipes of Kashmiri cuisine. Robust with flavours of browned onions, various spices and yoghurt, it is a very healthy low-fat dish. Dark red in colour and thin in consistency.
46. **Roth**: It is type of roti that is sweet and made of flour ghee and sugar. The Kashmiri make it during auspicious days. The Kashmiri pundits make it during auspicious days as a ritual.
47. **Sarvari**: Rice with black gram, chick peas or peas.
48. **Sevaiyaan**: It is a specialty of the Kashmir valley. Made with vermicelli and milk this dish is especially made during Eid celebrations.
49. **Shabdegh**: Mutton cooked with turnip.
50. **Sheer Chai**: Sheer Chai also known as Noon Chai or Pink Tea, is a traditional tea beverage of Kashmir. It is made of special tea leaves and a pinch of baking soda to give it a more pronounced pink color. It is slightly salty in taste.
51. **Shufta**: Shufta is Kashmiri dessert that is made up of a lot of dry fruits and sugar.
52. **Shufta Kanaguchhi**: It is a thick concoction of cottage cheese, dry fruits, saffron, milk, desi ghee and morel mushrooms from Srinagar.
53. **Skyu**: Skyu is thumb sized small pieces of wheat flour or aata, cooked in sufficient quantity of water or gravy.
54. **Sund panjeeri**: It is whole-wheat flour fried in sugar and ghee, heavily laced with dried fruits and herbal gums.
55. **Tabak maaz**: twice-cooked lamb ribs, initially braised with ground spices and milk, then browned in clarified butter.
56. **Tangdur**: A buttermilk with fresh wild vegetables.
57. **Tarkira**: Broken wheat Halwa- specialty of Jammu.
58. **Tehar**: It is a kind of Kashmiri turmeric rice that has a distinct yellow color. It is due to saffron added to the rice. The saffron gives the rice its

color and the distinct taste.

59. **Thenthuk:** A noodle soup prepared with wheat flour dough, mixed vegetables, and some pieces of mutton or Yak meat are added to enhance its taste and value.
60. **Thukpa:** Thukpa is a thick noodle-based soup with vegetables.
61. **Timatar Goli:** Meat balls cooked in tomato gravy
62. **Toda:** It is made from maize or bajra flour or rice flour. Flour is wetted with warm water and is constantly rubbed with the palm. It is then rounded, flattened and baked on tawa.
63. **Tsachvaru:** They are sesame-sprinkled leavened wheat breads, round in shape
64. **Tsoek Tsarvan:** Kidney or liver of lamb cooked delicately with assorted spices
65. **Yakhni:** Lamb cooked in yoghurt based .gravy. Yakhni is flavoured with *mawal* flowers, black and green cardamoms, onion paste and dry mint leaves with aromatic fennel seeds. Semi-thick light yellow gravy.

CHAPTER NINE

Festivals and Fairs of Jammu & Kashmir

"Kashmir is known as the paradise on Earth and rightly so. It has its charm in the enchanting valley views and green nature, but its cultural occasions and festivals add an extra flavour to the beauty of the state. Every occasion is celebrated with great zeal and zest, fancy feasting and incredible merry-making."

Listed here are some of the exclusive occasions:

Spitok Gutor Zanskar: Spitok Gutor Zanskar or Karsha Gustor Festival is is a mixture of colors, music, dance and message of victory of 'good over evil.' The largest monastery Zanskar, Karsha monastery (largest Geluk-pa (Yellow Hat) monastery) hosts this festival for two long days. Lamas offer friendly greetings to curious tourists, which is followed by a black hat dance performance. According to the locals, the dance is performed to ward off the evil forces and to establish the victory of good over the evil. The hat dancers are the symbols of divinities (Dharmapalas), and the patrons of the Geluk-pa order. Then the mask dancers perform the *Chaam*. At the end of the dance, statue of the evil forces is also burned to mark the end of the festival.

Thiksay Gustor: It is a two day festival that takes place in Ladakh. It is one of the many variable monastic festivals that take place in Ladakh, Jammu and Kashmir. The word 'Gustor' means literally sacrifice of the 29th date. The Thiksay Gustor festival takes place at the different monasteries of Spituk, Thiksay and Karsha Zanskar.

Matho Nagrang: Organized with fervor and joy, Matho Narang indeed the most colorful festival of Monasteries is an important festival organized in the valley of Ladakh in Jammu and Kashmir. This festival is held in Matho Narang Monastery and is celebrated on the 15th day of the first month of the Tibetan Calander. During this festival, monks clad in unusual dress of colorful and vibrant silk brocaded robes and masks, put up splendid performances during the eventful depicting various forms of God and Goddesses.

Galdan Namchot: It is mainly celebrated to commemorate the birthday and the Buddhahood of the Tibetan saint-scholar, Tsongkhapa. Tsongkhapa was the founder of the Gelukpa School that preached Tibetan Buddhism during the 14th century. In the later years, this Gelukpa School emerged as a major and dominant monastic order in the central Tibet region.

Losar: King Jamyang Namgyal , on the eve of setting out on an expedition against the Balti forces in winter was advised not to lead an expediting before the next year. To solve the problem, keeping the regard of the advice, he preponed the New Year celebrations in Ladakh by two months. This became established as a tradition and since then the Losar is celebrated on the first day of the eleventh month of every year.

Urs: The Urs (or Ziarats) is a typical Kashmiri festival. It is held annually at the shrines of Muslim saints on their death anniversaries. There is a saying " It snows when the Urs of Meesha Sahib is held, it is windy when the Urs of Batamol Sahib takes place, it rains on the occasion of the Urs of Bahauddin". These Urs are popular despite the rigours of weather. This is celebrated in different parts of Srinagar, not only by Muslims but Hindus and Sikhs also. An interesting feature of the Urs celebrations at Batamaloo (the locality in Srinagar named after the saint Batamol Sahib) and in Anantag (Rishi Mol's anniversary) is that both Muslims and Hindus abstain from taking meat during the course of the festival. The anniversary of Rishi Pir, a Hindu saint, held on the fifth day of the full moon of Baisakh, at his home in Srinagar is attended by Muslims also. The inter-communal participation is the main feature of the Urs celebrations.

Eid ul Azha and Eid ul Fitr: These are the two most important festivals for the people belonging to Muslim community in this _Paradise on Earth'. Eid-ul-Fitr marks the end of the fasting period of Ramadan. During this day Muslims end their fasts, wear new clothes and offer namaz six times instead of five. They celebrate this wonderful occasion by indulging themselves in grand feasts. Eid-ul-Adha is majorly a sacrifice day when people sacrifice their goats, sheep and share the meat with their families, neighbours, friends and poor people.

Hemis Festival: Hemis Festival is the most important festival in Ladakh region. The festival is to commemorate the birth anniversary of Guru Padmasambhava. The festival is organized in the huge courtyard of the largest monastery in Ladakh. The festival is celebrated on the 9th, 10th and 11th day of 5th month according to the Tibetan calendar. To portray this, Lamas and lay persons dress themselves in traditional clothes and century old masks, and perform a ritual dance (*Cham Dance*) depicting the victory of good over evil.

Baisakhi : The festival is celebrated on the 13th of April every year. This is a prominent Sikh festival but since the population of Sikhs is quite large in parts of Jammu and Kashmir as well, you will see the enthusiastic celebrations of this festival. The day is also famous as the birthday of the tenth Sikh Guru, Guru Gobind Singh. Marriage ceremonies during this period are a common phenomenon. Many people also take holy dip in the rivers. *Bhangra* Punjabi dance is very popular during this festival.

Tulip Festival: With hundreds of Tulip Gardens in all of Kashmir, the state flourishes with Tulips during the spring season. With the largest Tulip Garden in Asia in its bounty, Srinagar plays host to the great Tulip Festival every year. The festival boasts of the variety of Tulips garnered here. During the springs, the sight of the tulips in any of these gardens is a sight to behold, undoubtedly a mesmerizing and breathtaking sight, especially for a non-Kashmiri. Tulip Festival takes place at the Indira Gandhi Memorial Tulip Garden in Srinagar, Kashmir. The festival features a showcase of local handicrafts, luscious cuisine, cultural programs and of course, Tulips!

Shikara Festival: The lifeline and identity of the Dal Lake in Kashmir, Shikara needs to be celebrated once in a year. To promote tourism, Kashmir's government began this festival in 2016. During the festival, Shikaras are painted and dressed beautifully. Shikaras participate in Shikara Race, Dragon Boat Race and Canoe Polo Match. Other cultural programs are also organised which will give you a glimpse of the culture of Kashmir. It takes place in the months of July or August.

Gurez Festival: Around 123 km from the capital of Kashmir, Gurez is the placid valley in the Himalayas at an elevated height of about 8,000 feet. The picturesque valley has a plethora of scenic views as it lies on the ancient Silk Route. Neelum River flows amidst the Gurez valley and is a perfect destination for river rafting activity. The valley is an ideal place for trekking, zorbing, cycling, etc. People of Gurez play host to the annual festival in which they showcase their dance, handicrafts, cuisines, and culture.

Sindhu Darshan Festival: This festival is celebrated to honor the River Indus, which is locally known as the Sindhu River. It is believed that India has derived its name from this river. The Indus River is one of the longest rivers in the world. Indus is a trans-Himalayan The River has its source in southwestern Tibet and it flows into the Indian Territory near Leh in Ladakh. Sindhu is basically a Sanskrit word and the name of this mighty river is mentioned in the Rig Veda, that is one of the earliest chronicles of ancient India.

Lohri: Lohri also known as Makar Shankranti is an important Hindu Festival. Every year it is celebrated on 13th January to welcome the oncoming Spring Season. The celebration generally takes place at night when people gather around a huge bonfire. People sing, dance, exchange sweets and throw rice into the fire on this auspicious day. Jammu and Kashmir has many holy rivers and people are said to take a bath in these rivers to cleanse their soul for this festival. In the rural areas it is celebrated with much more joy and enthusiasm. In rural areas it is celebrated a little differently as young kids get gifts and spend time with newlyweds and new parents also receive gifts for their new born child. Young boys perform a special type of dance on Lohri called *Chajja Dance* which is quite entertaining and fun.

Navratra Festival: Though the yatra to the shrine of Mata Vaishno Devi is a round-the- year event, the one undertaken during the Navratras is considered the most auspicious. In order to showcase and highlight the regional culture, heritage and traditions of the area during this period, the State Tourism Department has instituted the Navratra Festival as an annual event to be held during September / October for all the nine auspicious days of the Navratras. A large number of tourists pay their obeisance to the deity during this period. This festival showcases the religious traditions as well as the popular culture of the region among the millions of pilgrims who visit the Vaishno devi Shrine during this period.

Dussehra: The festival of Dusshera is celebrated extravagantly in Jammu and Kashmir. On this day the war weapons and instruments are hallowed and after that they open a campaign. Three gigantic figures of Ravana, Meghnada and Kumbhkarana are made and stuffed with gun powder and fire crackers. These figures are placed in the center of a large open ground where the people of the city can gather and watch the burning ceremony of the demons. Little kids dress up like Ram, Sita and Lakshman, the characters from Ramayana. There is also a play depicting the whole story of Ramayana.

This festival is celebrated the victory of truth over evil.

Diwali: Jammu thrives with Hindus whose main festival of the year is Diwali. It is celebrated in the month of November and is also known as the festival of lights. People dress up in new clothes, light diyas and candles and play with fire crackers. As Diwali is the most important Hindu festival of the year it is celebrated with extra enthusiasm in Jammu and Kashmir as well.

FAIRS:

Several fairs are organized during the year some of them are described as under:

Mansar Food and Craft Mela: Stretching for three days, Mansar Food and Craft Mela is celebrated at the Mansar Lake, which is 60 km from Jammu. The fair is organized by Jammu and Kashmir Tourism Department in the month of April. It is the best place to see and buy beautiful handicrafts of the state.

Purmandal Mela: The religious fair of Purmandal is dedicated to Lord Shiva and goddess Parvati. Held in the month of February/ March on the auspicious occasion of Shivratri, the fair celebrates the marriage of Lord Shiva to Goddess Parvati. The mela lasts for three days.

Jhiri Mela: Held in the month of October/ November, Hiri Mela commemorates the courage of an honest farmer who preferred to give his life rather than getting defeated by the wickedness of the local landlord. He used to live in a village named Jhiri. The Mela earned its name from the village.

Bahu Mela: The beautiful Kali temple in the Bahu Fort serves as a venue for the wonderful Bahu Mela. The fair is held twice a year in March/April and September/October.

Vaishno Devi: Vaishno Devi is a temple of Vaishno Mata who is a form of Maa Durga. The temple of Vaishno Devi is situated 14 kilometers away from the town of Katra. Vaishno Devi is one of the most popular temples in India and the Vaishno Devi festival one of the most important festivals of India. Unlike other Indian festivals the festival of Vaishno Devi lasts for three months that is from September to December.

Amarnath yatra: Amarnath yatra is the most revered pilgrimage in Hinduism, one which every Hindu aspires to embark on once in his lifetime. This religious Yatra is organized every year to the great Himalayas to pay obience to holy tour of the scenic snow made Amarnath linga in the cave.

The Yatra can be undertaken along two routes- Baltal to Amarnath Cave and Pahalgam to Amarnath cave.

Chaitre Chaudash: Chaitre Chaudash is celebrated at Uttar Dehni, about 45 kms from Jammu in the month of March or April.

Kashmiri kitchen during festivals:

On normal days, the cooking, in both Hindu and Muslim homes, is mostly done on a *Dan*. A big dinner, called a *Sal*, or a *Wazawan*, is still cooked in a *Vurabal* which is an open-air kitchen. The fire-place, for this sort of cooking, is called a *Vura*. It is about 10' to 15 ' in length. In the shape of an above-ground drain, with air holes on both sides, it is built with bricks or stones. Fire-wood is used as fuel. Heat of such fires is very easily regulated for mass cooking. It is very convenient for deep and slow frying in big iron Cauldrons called *'Kadhais'*, as well as, for slow cooking and simmering, in earthenware pots especially. Here also the contents in cooking vessels are conveniently watched and stirred with different types of wooden or metallic ladles. Such low-level Vura also facilitates the time to time addition of ingredients. Generally, an hour or so before serving most of the dishes, the cooking vessels are removed from the Vura and are kept on charcoal or dry cowdung slow fires, for maturing of flavours and arriving at the right consistency of gravy, and also the desired 'texture'.

Among Kashmiri Pandits cooking of most Vegetarian and Non-vegetarian Dishes, is done mostly in pots made of baked clay. The pot is called a *Deg*, a *Degul* or a *Leij* according to its shape and size. Muslims cook generally in tinned copper pots.

The Kashmiri day begin at the crack of dawn while a delicate mist still hovers over the lakes. The first order of business in most homes is the setting of the samovars. Water is poured in and some live charcoal thrown into its' chimney. Once the water is boiling loose green tea is sprinkled in and a little sugar. Some crushed cardamom and almonds is also added. This is called Kahwa. It is drunk for breakfast and sipped all through the day.

Waazwan:

The Kashmiri muslim community banquet, 'waazwan', named for the 'waaza' or professional cooks, who prepare it, begins with the appearance of an unlikely procession. A team of about twenty or thirty chefs and assistants forms the team to cook waazwan. Their recipes are kept secret, locked away in their heads. The wazwan is led as a festival in its own & it is like a dream of every Muslim to have a wazwan organized.

Consumption of mutton has a very high regard in wazwan. Comprising of thirty-six courses, fifteen to thirty dishes of Wazwan are varieties of meat. Many of the delicacies are cooked through the entire night under the expert supervision of a *Vasta Waza* or head chef, assisted by an entourage of wazas under him. Kashmir's most formal meal, Wazwan is not only a ritual but also a ceremony. Traditionally, no spoons, forks or knives are used for eating food. Eaten with fingers, getting invited to a Wazwan is a rare luxury that one can enjoy these days.

The animals are slaughtered according to the Muslim custom and then butchered expertly on the spot. According to 'waaza' there are seventy two parts of an animal and a most of them are cooked. Organ meats such as kidneys, hearts, liver will be served for the host family for lunch.

Tents are set up, one as the kitchen and one as the dining pavilion. Earnest young men will cut meat into cubes, mince it and pound it repeatedly into a smooth paste. All of this; is done with mallets and cleavers over several hours.

When cooking is finished, long white sheets called 'dastarkhans', are spread on the carpeted floor of dining pavilion. Guests come in quietly and take their places, the men segregated from women. Jugs of water and basins are brought in so hands may be washed. A beautiful *Tasht – t – Nari* may also be presented and the guests to wash their hands as ritual.

It is time for food. This comes in covered *'tramis'* plates that are large enough to seat four people around them. The cover (sarposh) is removed; the name of God invoked with the cry of 'bismillah'

and the eating begins. The centre of the trami, heaped with rice, quartered by four seekh kababs and contains four pieces of methi korma, one tabak maaz, one safed murg, one zafrani murg, and the first few courses. The lids of tramis are whisked-off to release the most deliciously appetizing aromas of Wazwan. Yogurt is served in large clay bowls and sweet pumpkin chutney in saucers.

Other tramis may also follow who are also centered with a mojnd of rice in the center and other dishes surround it. One has to carve out his portion by cleanly using the finger tips to get the most exciting taste of 'rista' - spongy meatballs, 'raganjosh' - meatcubes cooked with yoghurt red chillies and saffron, 'palag korma' - tiny meatballs in a spinach sauce , 'ruangan tsaman' - fresh cheese chunks cooked with tomatoes, or goshtaba - large silky meatballs.

Seven Mandatory Dishes of Wazwan:

There are seven items that must be served in such occasions:

1. **Tabakhmaaz** or Qabargaah, barbecued lamb ribs prepared with milk, butter and ground spices
2. **Rista**, a spicy gravy preparation of meat balls where the ingredients of the gravy includes fennel, saffron and paprika and takes its colour from the dyer's alkanet
3. **Damiwal Korma**, a preparation of lamb roasted with spices, onion puree and yogurt and garnished with coriander leaves
4. **Rogan Josh**, one of the signature dishes of Kashmiri cuisines, a lamb gravy, ingredients of which includes asafoetida , Kashmiri chillies, yogurt, ginger and bay leaves among others.
5. **Gushtaba**, a preparation of spicy yogurt gravy containing meatballs
6. **Marchhwangan Korma**, a preparation of chicken thigh or leg pieces that is cooked with a spicy onion sauce
7. **Aab Gosh**, chunk of lamb prepared with thickened milk, cardamom and fennel-based spice mixture.

CHAPTER TEN

Classical Recipes from the J&K Kitchens

Out of the several dozen classical recipes it was a very difficult job to choose the best ones for you. I have tried to do so based on my experience and intercations with the local and traditional kitchen keepers. 12 recipes are presented hereby:

1. Narangi shorba

Ingredients:

- Fresh orange juice 1 cup
- Carrots peeled and chopped 3 medium
- Red pumpkin (bhopla/kaddu) deseeded and chopped 500 grams
- Onion roughly chopped 1 medium
- Green chillies roughly chopped 2
- Cumin seeds roasted and powdered 1 teaspoon
- Salt to taste
- Fresh cream ½ cup
- Fresh coriander leaves a few sprigs

Method:

- Boil chopped carrots, red pumpkin, onion, green chillies in one cup of water.
- Cook on medium heat for eight to ten minutes or till the vegetables are soft.
- Cool the cooked vegetables slightly and make a puree in the blender.

- Add roasted cumin powder, salt and one cup of water to the vegetable puree and bring to a boil.
- Reduce heat, add fresh orange juice and simmer for two to three minutes.
- Stir in fresh cream and serve hot garnished with fresh coriander leaves.

2. Aab Gosht

Ingredients:

- 250- ml.Milk
- 1 tea spoon-Cardamom crushed
- 3 numbers- Cloves
- 3 numbers-Cardamom
- 1 number-Mace
- Salt- To taste
- 1 tablespoon-Fennel powder
- 1 tea spoon-Ginger powder
- 4 numbers-Garlic crushed
- 500 grams-Mutton
- ½ cup-Brown onion paste
- ½ tea spoon-Pepper powder
- 2 tablespoons-Ghee
- Water - as required.

Method:

- In a bowl add water, mutton, crushed garlic, ginger powder, fennel powder, salt, mace, cardamom, cloves and mix it and put the lid on let it cook till the meat is tender.
- In a bowl add milk, crushed cardamom, boil this reduce the milk half.
- Heat ghee in another pan add brown onion paste, mutton pieces, cook it for some time.
- Add pepper powder, salt, pour the reduced milk and mutton stock, cook this for 5 minutes in a slow flame, then switch off the flame.

3. Ambal

Ingredients:

- 250 gm pumpkin (Orange coloured)
- 4-5 TbspTamarind paste
- 3 tbspJaggery, powdered
- ½ tsp fenugreek seeds
- 1 tsp ginger, chopped
- 1 tsp cumin seeds
- 4-5 Kashmiri dried red chillies
- 2-3 tsp turmeric powder
- 2 tbsp refined oil
- Salt for taste
- Red chilli powder, just a pinch
- Water
- Coriander leaves; to garnish

Method:

- First of all, cut the pumpkin into medium sized cubes.
- Now, in order to make the tamarind paste, soak the dried tamarind (easily available at grocery stores) in warm water. Immerse it completely in the water for about 10 minutes.
- Squeeze out the pulp and remove the seeds. Your tamarind paste is ready to use.
- Take a pan; add oil, fenugreek seeds, cumin seeds and ginger. Let them splutter for a while.
- Add red chillies, turmeric, salt, red chilli powder in the pan and sauté for half a minute.
- Now add pumpkin cubes and toss properly. Add tamarind paste and jaggery. Cook for 3-4 minutes on high flame.
- Add ½ cup water, cover the utensil with a lid and cook (on a low flame) till the pumpkin is soft and almost 'mash-able'. Garnish your dish with coriander leaves.

4. Kulath ki khatti dal

Ingredients:

- 1 cup Horse Gram Dal (Kollu/ Kulith) , washed and soaked
- 1 Green Chilli, slit
- 1 inch Ginger
- 1 tbsptamarind paste
- 4 cloves Garlic , crushed
- ½ teaspoon Turmeric powder (Haldi)
- 1 teaspoon Kashmiri red chilli powder
- Salt , to taste
- 1 tablespoon Rice flour
- 3 tablespoons Water
- 1 tablespoon Ghee
- 1 teaspoon Cumin seeds (Jeera)
- ½ teaspoon Asafoetida (hing)
- 2 sprig Coriander (Dhania) Leaves , finely chopped

Method:

- Wash and soak the horse gram for about 20 minutes.
- Heat a pressure cooker on medium flame, add the drained horsegram along with 2 cups of water.
- To the horsegram add the slit green chilli, ginger, garlic, salt, turmeric powder and red chilli powder.
- Close the pressure cooker and pressure cook for 6-8 whistles and turn off the flame.
- Allow the pressure to release naturally and then open the pressure cooker.
- Mash the Kulith ki dal with the back of a ladle and set aside.
- In a mixing bowl, combine the rice flour with water to make a slurry.
- In another pan, heat ghee on medium-low flame, once hot, to this add the cumin seeds and asafoetida and allow it to sizzle. To this add the cooked and mashed Kulith Ki Dal and bring to a single boil.
- Once the Kashmiri Kulith ki dal comes to a single boil, gradually add in the rice flour slurry and give it a quick stir.

- When you see the Kashmiri Kulith ki dal begin to thicken, add the tamarind paste, bring to single boil ,turn off the flame and add the finely chopped coriander leaves.
- Serve hot.

5. Modur Pulao

Ingredients:

- 1 cup Basmati rice
- 1 cup Sugar
- 6 tablespoons Ghee
- 3 Bay leaves (tej patta)
- 6 Cloves (Laung)
- 1 inch Cinnamon Stick (Dalchini)
- 6 Cardamom (Elaichi) Pods/Seeds
- ¼teaspoon Whole Black Peppercorns
- ¼teaspoon Saffron strands
- 1 teaspoon tablespoon Dates, chopped
- 1 teaspoon tablespoon Badam (Almond), blanched
- 1 teaspoon teaspoon Cashew nuts, chopped
- 1 teaspoon teaspoon Raisins
- Salt, as required
- 3 cups Water

Method:

- To begin making the Modur Pulao Recipe, wash rice thoroughly with water and soak for half an hour. Drain the water and set aside.
- In a small bowl, soak saffron with a tablespoon of water.
- In a small saucepan, add 2 cups of water and bring it to boil. Add rice and cook for about 5 to 10 minutes. Ensure that the rice is only cooked ¾ th. Do not cook for long time.
- Drain water from the rice and set aside.
- In a non-stick kadai heat ghee over medium flame. Once the ghee is hot, lower the flame and add cloves, bay leaves, cinnamon stick, cardamom, and Peppercorns.

- Cook them until peppercorns clutter.
- Now, add sugar, ½ cup of water and cook until they dissolve completely. It should be in thick syrup consistency. Add the half cooked rice and give it a stir.
- Now add chopped dates, raisins, almonds and cashews to the rice. Soak dates and almonds in warm water for few minutes for chopping it without efforts.
- Combine them well and pour the saffron water on top of the rice.
- Cover the pan and cook rice over low flame for about 20 to 25 minutes until they are cooked well. Ensure to stir them occasionally to prevent it from being burnt at the bottom
- In case if you have added undercooked rice, add required amount of water. Ensure to check the consistency of the rice often to avoid overcooking
- Serve Modur Pulao warmly to satisfy your sweet tooth. Serve Modur Pulao along with Kashmiri Style Dum Aloo and Phulkas for a weekend lunch.

6. Shufta

Ingredients:

- Cottage cheese ¾ cup
- Almonds ¼cup
- Dates dried ¼cup
- Coconut ¼
- Apricots ¼ cup
- Walnuts ¼ cup
- Cashewnuts ¼cup
- Raisins ¼cup
- Saffron (kesar) ½ teaspoon
- Ghee to deep fry
- Green cardamom powder ¼teaspoon
- Cinnamon powder ¼teaspoon
- Dry ginger powder (soonth) ½ teaspoon
- Black pepper powder ½ teaspoon
- Sugar 1 ½ cups

- Rose petals for garnish

Method:

- Cut the cottage cheese into half inch sized cubes. Soak the almonds in one cup of hot water for five minutes.
- Drain, peel and halve them. De-seed dates and chop them roughly. Chop the coconut into small pieces. De-seed the apricots and cut into small pieces.
- Chop walnuts and cashewnuts into small pieces. Wash raisins and pat them dry. Soak saffron in one teaspoon of water.
- Soak the almonds, raisins, cashewnuts, dry dates, apricots, walnuts and coconut pieces in two cups water for about half an hour.
- Heat ghee in a wok and deep-fry the cottage cheese cubes till golden brown. Drain and keep aside.
- Transfer the soaked nuts and coconut in a pan and bring to a boil.
- Reduce heat Add the saffron, cardamom powder, cinnamon powder, ginger powder, pepper powder and sugar to the soaked nuts and cook on low heat till the syrup thickens two thread consistency.
- Stir in the cottage cheese pieces and cook for a minute. Serve garnished with rose petals.

7. Chhang

Ingredients:

- 5 cups -flavorful rice
- The normal amount of water you would use to cook your rice.
- 1 full tablespoon - dry powdered yeast or chanzi .

Method:

- Cook the rice.
- Once the rice is cooked, stir around the rice in the rice cooker or pot to loosen it .
- Spread the rice onto a very clean working surface to cool it. Work through the rice when it is cool enough to touch, loosening up any

clumpy bits.

- When the rice is tepid warm, sprinkle the yeast all over and mix well.
- Pour the rice mixture in a dry clean large container.
- Cover it with a lid.
- Swaddle it like a baby in a couple of warm blankets.
- Leave it 4-5 days in a warm place without opening it, so that it can ferment well and release strong alcoholic odour.
- Once the chhang is done, transfer it to another clean container, and add about 3 cups of water, and then put it in the refrigerator.
- Wait again for 24 hours so that the chhang rests.
- Serve in small glasses as drinks.

8. Roganjosh

Ingredients:

- 500 grams - Mutton, with bones, cut into medium pieces
- 1 cup - Curd
- Salt - as required
- Mustard oil - as required For whole spices
- 2 - Black cardamom)
- 4 - Green cardamom
- 4 - Cloves
- 1 inch - Cinnamon Stick
- 1 - Bay leaf
- ½ - teaspoon Black pepper powder
- 1 - teaspoon Fennel Powder
- ½ - teaspoon Asafoetida
- 2 - teaspoons Kashmiri red chilli powder
- ½ - inch Ratan jot (alkanet), (infuse it in heated oil) For marination
- 1 - teaspoon Fennel seeds
- ¼ - teaspoon Cinnamon Powder
- 1 - teaspoon Kashmiri red chilli powder
- ½ - teaspoon Black pepper powder
- ½ - teaspoon Cardamom Powder

Method:

- To begin making the Kashmiri Rogan Josh recipe, wash mutton nicely and drain water completely.
- Marinade the mutton with mentioned Ingredients under Marination for approximately for 1 and 1-½ hours. Cling wrap the bowl and refrigerate it for better results.
- Heat oil in a heavy bottomed wok and add bay leaf and other whole spices mentioned.
- Immediately, add marinated mutton and mix well. Fry on medium to high flames stirring occasionally.
- Now add asafoetida and stir well. Add almost 1 cup of water in the mutton mix and allow it to cook with lid closed.
- In a separate bowl, add yogurt and red chilli powder and fennel powder and whisk nicely.
- Take off the lid and add whisked yogurt and mix well such that everything incorporates nicely. Adjust salt as needed.
- Now add Ratan Jot / root infused in oil in the mutton and cook till mutton is soft and tender. Garnish with fresh coriander and serve hot.
- Serve Kashmiri Rogan Josh with hot steamed rice or rumali rotis for a delicious weekend meal.

9. Ladyar-tsaman

Ingredients:

- 1 kg - Paneer
- 2 table spoons - Fennel powder
- 1 table spoon - Turmeric powder
- Salt - to taste
- 1 tea spoon - Ginger powder
- 1 tea spoon - Cumin powder
- 2-3 - rushed Black Cardamom
- 3-5 - crushed Green Cardamom
- ½ tea spoon - Black Cumin
- Pinch - Hing
- 2 - Tej Patte
- 1 cup - Milk
- 3-4 table spoons - Mustard oil

Method:

- Fry the paneer / cottage cheese a day prior and put it in a vessel containing salt, turmeric powder and some ice cold water and ice cubes and put in refrigerator overnight.
- When you want to cook the dish, take out the vessel with the paneer and masalas from the refrigerator and keep it aside to remain under room temperature.
- Add fennel powder, ginger powder, turmeric, salt, hing and bay leaves in a bowl, mix well and keep aside.
- Heat some mustard oil in a pan and fry the paneer/ cottage cheese till golden- brown. Put it into the vessel containing spices.
- Now add the paneer with the masalas to the pan and cook it on low flame till only one glass of curry is left.
- Crush some black cumin between your palms and add into the pan with some green cardamom, black cardamom and milk.
- Cook this curry for another ten minutes on low flame and serve with rice.

10. Kofta Dilpasand

Ingredients:

For koftas:

- 250 gm - Mince mutton
- 50 gm - Mince lard
- ½tsp - Red chili pdr.
- ¾ tsp - Garam masala pdr.
- 1 tsp - Ginger paste
- 1tsp - Oil/ ghee
- 1-2 nos - Gr. Chilies chopped
- 2 cups - Curd
- 3 tbsp- Khoya
- ¼ tsp Hing
- 1 tsp Saunf
- Salt - to taste
- ½ tsp - Jeera pdr.

Gravy:

- ¼ tsp - Hing
- 5 tsp - Ghee/ oil
- ½ cup - Curd
- ¼ tsp - Dhegi mirch
- ½ tsp – Salt
- ½ tsp -Dhania pdr. --
- ½ tsp - Jeera pdr. ---
- ½ tsp - Garam masala pdr.–
- ½ tsp - Saunf
- ¼ tsp - Sonth

Method:

- Mix together and beat well.
- Churn the mince along with the lard in a mixer and then rub with the palm of your hand.
- Mix together all the Ingredients mentioned under koftas.
- Mix well and form into 12 small balls.
- Mix all the masalas with curd and beat well.
- Heat oil / ghee, add hing, and fry for 1 minutes. Add beaten curd mixture with masalas. Go on stirring till it boils.
- Add koftas and 1¼ cups of water.
- Cook uncovered on high flame till koftas become firm, about 4-5 boils.
- Cover and cook on medium heat for 15-20 minutes, till koftas become tender and little gravy remains and oil floats on top.
- Serve hot.

11. Guchhi Biriyani

Ingredients:

- 5 cups - Rice
- ½ cup - Mushrooms

For the Filling:

- 2 tbsp- Paneer
- 2 tsp, chopped - Cashew nuts
- 2 tsp, chopped - Raisins
- 1 tsp, chopped - Ginger
- ½ tsp - Cumin seeds

For the Curry:

- ½ cup - Oil
- 2 tsp - Whole garam masala
- 1 cup - Onion Paste
- ¾ cup - Hung yoghurt
- 2 tbsp- Cashew nut paste
- 2 tbsp - Ginger garlic paste
  ½ tsp - Turmeric powder
- 1 tsp - Yellow chilli powder
- Salt - to taste

Method:

- Clean the mushrooms and keep aside.
- For the filling, mix together all the Ingredients and fill the mushrooms with the prepared filling.
- For the curry, heat oil in a pan.
- Add the garam masala and saute till it crackles.
- Add onion paste and cook till it leaves water.
- Stir in all the other Ingredients and cook for a few minutes.
- Remove and keep aside.
- Boil rice in sufficient water till three quarters done.
- Drain and keep aside.
- In a pot, spread alternate layers of rice, mushrooms and the prepared curry.
- Cover and cook on very low heat till the rice is done and the mushrooms are tender.
- Remove from heat.
- Serve hot.

12. Kesar Firni

Ingredients:

- 50 grams - Basmati rice soaked
- Few strands - Saffron
- 8-10 chopped - Pistachios
- 1 cup - Sugar
- ½ teaspoon - Green cardamom powder
- Few drops - Rose water

Method:

- Bring the milk to a boil in a deep pan.
- Lower the heat and let it simmer till it reduces a little. Grind the soaked rice to a coarse paste.
- Add a little milk to it and mix to make it a little thinner.

Part B: HIMACHAL PRADESH

(The Highlands of Lahaul, Spiti and the intense landscape of Himachal)

CHAPTER ELEVEN

Geography of Himachal Pradesh

Situated in the Western Himalayas, it is bordered by states of Jammu and Kashmir on the north, Punjab on the west, Haryana on the southwest, Uttarakhand on the southeast, and the Tibet autonomous region on the east. At its southernmost point, it also touches the state of Uttar Pradesh. The state's name was coined from the Sanskrit—*Him* means 'snow' and *achal* means 'land' or 'abode'—by acharya Diwakar Datt Sharma, one of the state's eminent Sanskrit scholars.

Himachal has everything which can fascinate a tourist. Mighty snow peaks, deep gorges, lush green and golden valleys, flower filled meadows, misty woods, fast flowing icy rivers, glaciers, gushing water streams, steep waterfalls, enchanting lakes, rippling streams are a few manifestations of its unparallel beauty.

Geographically the state is divided into three regions:-

(a) The Shivalik ranges (the height from plain upto 915 meters);

(b) Colder Zone (the height is about 4500 meters); and

(c) the Axis and Crystalline core of the whole system (the height above 4500 meters but below 5500 meters).

Due to extreme variation in elevation, great variation occurs in the climatic conditions of Himachal. The climate varies from hot and sub-humid tropical in the southern tracts to, with more elevation, cold, alpine, and glacial in the northern and eastern mountain ranges. The state's winter capital, Dharamshala receives very heavy rainfall, while areas like Lahaul and Spiti are cold and almost rainless. The Siwalik region has hot summers (April to June), with temperatures rising upto 38 °C, cool and dry winters (October to March), and a wet season (July to September), with rains brought by the southwestern monsoon. As elevations increase farther north, the climate becomes wetter and cooler. Snowfall is common in alpine tracts (generally above 2,200 meters (7,218 ft) i.e. in the higher and trans-Himalayan region). In the Great Himalayas, winters are bitterly cold and snowy, with temperatures dropping around -18 °C. The average rainfall is 152 cms. (60 inches).

Himachal Pradesh has many perennial snow-fed rivers and streams, in addition to four major watercourses. The eastern portion of the state is drained primarily by the Sutlej River, which rises in Tibet. Draining the western part of Himachal Pradesh is the Chenab (Chandra-Bhaga), Ravi, and Beas rivers, which have their source in the Great Himalayas. They are protected by an extensive cover of natural vegetation.

CHAPTER TWELVE

History of Himachal Pradesh

"Himachal Pradesh, popularly known as the land of Gods "Dev Bhoomi" has a glorious history, which dates back to around two million years. Initially the first inhabitants of the Himachal Pradesh occupied the foothills of the state. Later after the establishment of the Indus Valley Civilization in Himachal Pradesh, they were forced to shift their base from foothills to the upper areas of the hills. Dasas, Koilis, Halis, Dagis, Dhaugris, Khasas and Kinnars, the local tribes of Himachal Pradesh inhabited this land since the ancient times. Later many other clans, tribes and dynasties occupied the land of Himachal Pradesh."

The Aryans established their rule over Himachal Pradesh during the period before Rig Veda. The Aryans were very clever and through their strategies they defeated the local tribes and became the permanent inhabitants of Himachal Pradesh. During this period several small Janapadas or Republics were also established in the present Himachal Pradesh. Later, the Mauryans arrived and ruled by conquering most of the small republics. Ashoka was a famous king of this dynasty who after the terrible war took faith in Buddhism and propagated the Buddhist philosophy to help people become truly happy.

After the decline of the Mauryans, the entire land of Himachal Pradesh came under the control of small local chieftains known as the Thakurs or Ranas. Later in the seventh century, the Harsh became dominant and became the rulers of all the small kingdoms. The middle of the seventh century saw the rise of the Rajputs and they established small principalities in Himachal Pradesh. Then the foreign invaders made their presence felt by conquering several forts of Himachal Pradesh. Then came the turn of the

Mughals who were defeated by the hill rulers.

The Britishers who wanted to rule over India joined hands with the hill rulers and started to establish their rule in Himachal Pradesh. Initially the hill rulers supported the British. After 1914, the states of Himachal Pradesh started participating in the revolt against Britishers and finally in 1947 India became independent. After India became free in 1947, a number of princely hilly states were integrated into a single unit to be administered by the Government of India. Himachal Pradesh came into being as a state of the India Union on April 15, 1948, by integrating 31 big and small hill states of the region. In 1956, it was converted into a Union Territory. Subsequently, some more hill areas of the Punjab state were added to this Union Territory and it was made into a full-fledged state, the status that it continues to have now.

Demography: Himachal Pradesh is one of the least-urbanized states in India. In the early 21st century its urban population accounted for less than 10 percent of the total. There are more than 50 towns, and the capital, Shimla, constitutes a city of reasonable size. The capitals of the former princely states, including Bilaspur, Mandi, Chamba, and Kullu, are now district headquarters. Dalhousie, Kasauli, and Sabathu are hill resorts of British origin. Kangra, Palampur, Solan, and Dharmshala are other notable towns in the state.

Retaining their age-old customs and traditions, the people of Himachal Pradesh are proud of their rich cultural heritage. But at the same time they have embraced new influences keeping in pace with the changing times. Their passion for life clearly reflects in their colourful dresses and amazing celebrations. Reflecting unity in diversity, Himachal Pradesh is a land where different religions are followed and different languages are spoken. The beauty of the culture of Himachal Pradesh lies in its simplicity.

The most commonly spoken languages in Himachal Pradesh are Hindi, Punjabi, Pahari, Dogri, Kangri and Kinnauri. Hinduism is the main religion in Himachal Pradesh. The region being nestled in the Himalayas - the abode of the Hindu God Shiva and Goddess Parvati - there are numerous temples of Shiva and Parvati scattered all around the state.

The Hindu communities residing in Himachal include the Brahmins, Rajputs, Kannets, Rathis and Kolis. There are also tribal population in the state which mainly comprises Gaddis, Kinnars, Gujjars, Pangawals and Lahaulis. In some area, like Lahaul & Spiti, there is a majority of Buddhist population. A percentage of people are also Tibetans. Muslim,

Christian and Sikhs are in relatively small numbers. The physical feature of most of the people resemble the Aryans however, there are still many with prominent Mongoloid feature. Although rearing of goats, sheep and other cattle is an important occupation of the people of Himachal Pradesh, most of the population is dependent on agriculture for survival.

CHAPTER THIRTEEN

Climate and Agriculture of Himachal Pradesh

Climate:

The state of Himachal Pradesh, India is a hilly region and it experiences a pleasant Climate throughout the year. It even experiences heavy snow fall during the winter months. The weather of Himachal alters with the change of altitude. Summer lasts from April to June in Himachal Pradesh, and the temperature ranges between 5°C and 24°C keeping the air comforting during the peak daytime while it can sometimes drop down to about 3.2°C in the night time.

However, the climate is cooler than the mainland because of the high altitude, plenty of forests and fresh mountain breeze. Alpine zones of the north remain cool even during the peak of the summer, and some high mountains even receive snowfall during May. Monsoon begins in July and continues through September with a wide variation in average rainfall. Winter (October to February) in Himachal Pradesh is severe with heavy snow fall especially in the northern parts located high in the mountains.

Almost all of the state receives snowfall though it is not very heavy in the main cities. The temperature gets freezing with snowfall in several regions between 0°C to 13°C depending on the altitude.

Agriculture and staple food:

Agriculture contributes over 45% to the net state domestic product. It is the main source of income and employment in Himachal. Over 93% of the population in Himachal depends directly upon agriculture which provides direct employment to 71% of its people. The entire population of the state more or less depends directly upon the agriculture of Himachal Pradesh. The major portion of the revenue earning in the state's economy is carried out by the cash crops in the Himachal Pradesh agriculture.

The chief food crops cultivated in Himachal Pradesh agriculture include wheat, maize, rice, barley, seed-potato, ginger, vegetables, vegetable seeds, mushrooms, chicory seeds, hops, olives, and fig. Himachal Pradesh is also known as the *'Apple State of India'*. It, today, grows a variety of best apples in India including Red Delicious, Golden and Yellow Newton. With citrus in valleys, grapes in high hills, mangoes, litchis, strawberries, apricots, peaches, cherries, pears, Kiwi and olive in warmer and temperate regions altogether makes Himachal the *"Fruit Bowl of India"*. Fruit growing in Himachal is presently fetching over Rs.300 crore annually.

Special efforts are being made to promote cultivation of new crops like hops, pistachio nuts, sarda melon and saffron. The agricultural sector of Himachal Pradesh has adopted a diversification approach that demands for a focus on the production of off- season vegetables that include potato, ginger, soya bean, oilseeds, and pulses. T

he town of Solan is known as *'Mushroom City of India'* for growing button mushrooms. The naturally grown mushrooms in the forests, called *guchhi*, have no parallels in taste and guchhi-pulao, with guchhi fried ric and guchhi matar can easily be the prized gourmet item in any aristocracy.

Himachal is also said to be the flower basket of the country, with orchards being widespread. Meadows and pastures are also seen clinging to steep slopes. On the higher regions in the summer and in the winter season at the lower level, the hillsides and orchards bloom with wild flowers, while gladiolas, carnations, marigolds, roses, chrysanthemums, tulips and lilies are carefully cultivated.

Apart from agriculture, many are involved in different types of artistic production and handicraft produced in this state is worth appreciating. The most popular crafts produced in the villages of Himachal Pradesh include carpets, leather works, shawls, paintings, metalware, wood work, etc. Among these, the Pashmina shawl has earned popularity all over the country. The colourful Himachali caps are also a famous art work. Weaving, carving, chiselling, etc. are considered to be an integral part of the village life in Himachal Pradesh. The tribes are generally mountain dwellers whose main occupation is cattle rearing, goat and lamb rearing. These tribes are the major producer of milk in the state.

CHAPTER FOURTEEN

Important features of Himachali Cookery

The state of Himachal Pradesh has a vast basket of traditional foods of its own. People of the state have been following the method of preparation from their ancestors and these dishes have continued like a tradition in maximum parts of Himachal. Some of the traditional foods still form a staple diet while rest is prepared during special occasions. Most of the foods were prepared by boiling, roasting, smoking, frying and fermentation. The food patterns of the state are highly influenced by the availability of raw materials, geographical and climatic conditions. The state comprises of number of communities, races and cultures intermingled together. Thus, the preferred taste also varies from region to region.

> "*The cuisine has been influenced by Punjabi and Tibetian food style.*"

The staple foods of the people of Himachal Pradesh are rice, wheat and maize but one can find local variations due to the pattern of food production and altitudinal variation, e.g. in the barren regions of Lahaul spiti and Kinnaur, the local people consume the products having coarse grains (buckwheat, millet, barley) as the main substrate, while in the lower areas of the state (Kangra, Hamirpur, Bilaspur) people prefer roties (chapatis) made of rice or maize flour.

In the pasture dominated regions, milk and milk products are widely used. Irrespective of the regional differences in the dishes of the state, people have specific liking for non-vegetarian items cooked along with generous doses of spices and ghee.

The ethnic food of Himachal Pradesh is rich and varied, while relying heavily on local ingredients. It can be a healthy choice with a balanced diet of steamed rice or *roti*, lots of vegetables, *dal* (lentils), yogurt and *saag* (a spinach and/or mustard leaf based dish). Thus, the natives of the state consume a range of foods prepared from cereals, pulses, milk, fruits and vegetables.

A number of ethnic cereal based fermented and non fermented food preparations have been developed and consumed by the natives of the selected area. *Bhaturu and Marchu* are fermented and deep-fried bread made of refined flour. In district Mandi and Hamirpur, this fermented *roti* is fried after stuffing it either with thick and cooked paste of soybean or black gram (kala chana) and is termed as *Beduan roti. Bhaturu* is the staple diet while *beduan* is prepared during festivals or on some special occasions. Similarly in Kangra district *Babroo* is prepared from rice or wheat flour slurry. The procedure of making the *babroo* is similar to that of preparing *dosa*. Preparation of salty *Babroos* is common in Lahaul & Spiti area of Himachal Pradesh. In Hamirpur, sweet *Babroos* are prepared and named as *Dhandar*.

Natives of district Mandi prepare *Chilru* in the same manner as Bhatura, but only the wheat flour is replaced by rice flour to which only water is added till the batter reaches a liquid consistency. They are termed as *Chareli* in Hamirpur. The *Chilru* are served along with black gram *dal* (broth) or milk. *Patende*, a sort of pancake prepared from rice flour is popular in Hamirpur and Chamba districts. In Lahaul Spiti valley, the leaves of buckwheat are mixed with wheat flour and made into cakes called, *Aktori*. Similarly *tiskori* and *mangjangkori* are thick *rotis* prepared from bran of wheat and buckwheat grains. *Tchog* is a special kind of food prepared during religious ceremonies. Another dish from this region is *Siddu*, which is a traditionally fermented steam cooked oval or disc shaped dish prepared with refined flour. *Marchu / Poltu / Pole* are salted roties deep fried (in mustard oil) prepared in Lahaul Spiti and Kinnaur districts, especially during the tribal festivals of Phagli, Halda and marriage ceremonies.

The sweet snacks of the state comprises of *Rot* made from dough of wheat flour and jaggery especially in the areas of Una, Hamirpur and Bilaspur. It is used for *puja*/religious purpose. While in Mandi and Kangra districts, fermented wheat flour slurry is used to make oval shape balls called *Gulgulae/malpude/babroo* (sweet fritters). These are specially prepared during birthday ceremony. *Mithdoo* or *sancholoo* is another popular sweet dish from Hamirpur made from wheat flour, ghee and grated coconut.

Another cereal based preparation is *Seera* which is famous in Mandi, Kangra, Bilaspur and Hamirpur. There is a tradition of gifting *seera* to the bride from her parent's during her marriage. All these sweet snacks are prepared during religious, birthday, festive or marriage ceremonies.

The beautiful state of Himachal Pradesh provides one with a wide range of lip smacking and delicious food items. One among them is *Pahari madra. Madra* is a rich dish of lentils made with yoghurt. Mostly soaked and boiled chick peas (*Kabuli chana)* or red kidney beans or black eyed beans (*raungi)* are used. Another tasty dish in Kangra, Mandi, Chamba, Hamirpur and Bilaspur is crispy Mah *ki dal ke pakoru.* These are fried discs with hole in the centre. *Dahin Bhalla* is prepared by the same method where these *pakorus* are termed as *bhalla* and no spice or salt is added to them. These *bhallas* are put in spiced curd after dipping in lukewarm water so as to make them soft.

Dried balls having a diameter of about 3-8 cm named *Badi* is used as an adjunct for cooking vegetables, grains or legumes. *Chawal ke atte* (Rice flour) *ki beduan roti* is a baked cereal Black gram is used as a base material for many of the dishes and *Sepubari/Mukandbari* is one more addition to the list of such dishes where black gram is the main ingredient.

Livestock are an integral component of the agricultural production systems in Himachal Pradesh. Traditional milk based products are prepared from the milk of several species of indigenous cattle, buffalo, sheep, goats, and *churu* (hybrid of cow and yak). Curd locally called *dahin* acts as a supplementary food to the local diet of *a Himachali.* It is also called *noo* or *nuch* in Lahaul Spiti and *doyang* in Kinnaur. Another very popular by-product of milk is *chaa/ lassi* (buttermilk). It is the liquid leftover after extracting butter from churned yoghurt. It is consumed as a beverage and local people consider it to be a good digestive and carminative drink.

Nudu is a ceremonial food prepared by cooking wheat flour in milk with small amount of salt to be eaten with ghee. Similarly, *kulu* is made from buttermilk. *Tchaku cha* (salty butter tea) is an indigenous drink of Lahaul Spiti.

Chhaas or Chaa is used for preparing a delectable cuisine named *Kadi* using gram flour. In Kangra and Mandi, people enjoy the preparation with rice while in Hamirpur and Bilaspur, it is relished more with *roti/chapati* of maize flour and is termed as *Kadu.* Similarly *Khoru* is another dish which is prepared from buttermilk. Apart from being simply used as an ingredient for a dish, *Chaa* is also utilized as a medicine for treating digestive ailments/ disorders and a good example is *Redu*. It is a semi liquid drink which is served with a belief that it helps to give relief during indigestion.

In district Chamba, leaves of bicchu buti (wild nettle) are relished as vegetable. It is locally called as *Bicchu buti ka saag. Karalen or kachnaar ki sabzi* is another delicious wild vegetable consumed by the people during the month of March- April. *Bhey* or fried lotus stem are very popular and scrumptious snacks of this region.

Unripe fresh fruit of *Lasiare/lasora* is used to prepare vegetable or pickle after removing the stone and sticky white pulp. Another so-called neglected fern which is fully utilized by the rural people of the state is *Lungd,* It is an edible fern, available as long stocks with curled top and hairy growth over it.

In some areas of Mandi district, overnight soaked seeds of Indian hemp or *bhang/bhangolu* are ground to a fine paste and are utilized to prepare a local dish called *Bhangolu ki kadi. Bhruni ki sabji* is also popular among various wild vegetables relished by the Himachali people. This dish is prepared from tender leaves of fig. In Hamirpur, Bilaspur and Kangra a number of mouth watering dishes are prepared from the locally available mango. *Ambua* is prepared from the pulp of ripened mangoes. *Chhachaa* a sweet and sour chutney prepared from raw mangoes A semi-liquid dish named *Mahni* is also prepared from pulp extracted from boiled raw mangoes.

Among the tubers, colocasia is widely cultivated and is utilized to prepare a number of recipes. Pickles from vegetables and fruits like *lingri* (fern), bottle gourd, pear, peach, plum, *bidana, galgal,* brinjal, etc are prepared and consumed in various parts of the state especially in Kullu district. Colocasia is locally termed as *Kachalu* is alltime favourite and is used in many ways, such as Patrode which is a roll of colocasia leaves layered with mixture of gram flour and other spices. *Khati bhuji/ Garyali bhuji is* prepared from leaves, stem, and bulb of *Colocasia.* Stem portion of the colocasia plant is used to prepare *kaandal/khandole.*

Sura is millet based fermented beverage consumed during local festivals like *shoeri saja* and marriages in rural area in Kullu especially lug valley. *Chhang* is an indigenous rice beer made in the tribal belt of Lahaul & Spiti. It is a very popular traditional alcoholic drink consumed during marriages and other local festivals. It is an indispensable hospitality beverage among tribal of Lahaul valley, and is considered to provide protection against cold during winter months. Apart from these, various fruit based fermented beverages made from a number of local fruits are popular in Himachal Pradesh especially in Kinnaur district. *Chulli, angoori / kinnauri, arak/ara* and *rak* are prepared by fermentation of wild apricot, locally available grapes, apple / pear and wild almond respectively. These beverages have been a part of socio-cultural life of people in Kinnaur.

Dham is a sacred interesting and delicious meal prepared on festivals only by Brahmin chefs called 'botis'.

Non- vegetarian food:

Traditional foods and beverages in Himachal Pradesh using meat are very limited. *Juma* is a favorite dish of Lahaul Spiti prepared in winters. Wheat flour/millet flour is mixed with spices and this paste is stuffed in sheep intestines. This is then steam cooked and eaten hot with *chutney* or *tchati* (mutton soup). *Geri* or *shakhal* is large mutton pieces mixed with spices and cooked in water. It is also consumed during winters especially in local festivals (*phagli* or *halda*).Apart from this Kullu trout, grilled fishes, chicken anardana are very popular.

CHAPTER FIFTEEN

Cooking equipments of a traditional Himachali Kitchen

1. **Charoti/Batohi**- The big brass vessels with round bottom and slender neck with collar. These are used for cooking all dishes including rice.)
2. **Dabru** - Another brass ladle like container with a handle and a large bowl shape at one end. Dabru is used for stirring food and also for serving food to people invited for the treat.)
3. **Kadchhe** (The bigger ladle, but smaller than Dabru), used for serving in the feasts.
4. **Jug**- A flask made up of brass.
5. **Chhadolu** -a container made of weaved bamboo, which is used to serve rice. It is also used as a strainer for draining of the cooked rice. It is also used in draining washed pulses and vegetables.
6. **Khara**- bigger version of chhadolu, which contains almost 100 times the amount of rice a chhadolu can handle.
7. **Kadhai**- made of iron, may be of different sizes and used for cooking, frying and tempering.
8. **Chhabdi** – weaved bamboo basket to keep breads.
9. **Sil batta**- mortar and pestle.
10. **Palta**- big spatula made of iron.
11. **Chimta**- a flat and big twizzer used to hold vessels and in preparation of breads.
12. **Tenthu** or (palta) - a big spatula with long handed, used in stirring food.
13. **Sansi**- to hold vessels while cooking or to pickup hot food in the vessel.
14. **Chaklaa belan**- used to roll rotis and chapattis.
15. **Chhalni**- Sieve

16. **Thali**- generally brass or steel thalis are used. They can be used for serving food, having food, covering cooking vessels and also for keeping the raw materials.
17. **Parat**- big thali
18. **Glass**- water tumbler generally made of brass.
19. **Katoree**- bowl.
20. **Jhara**- strainer
21. **Degcha**-big cooking utensil like patila.
22. **Tawa**- flat round iron plate used to cook rotis and chapattis.
23. **Patila**- cylindrical vessels made of aluminum with or without handle, used to cook food.
24. **Buckets**- used to hold water and also used to serve food to the people sitting in the painth.
25. **Pattal**- leaf plates in which people eat food in painth.

CHAPTER SIXTEEN

Special Himachali dishes from festive occasions

1. **Aktori:** Aktori is prepared in the form of a cake or pancake made with the buckwheat leaves which is further cooked in the wheat flour. Although, the dish originates in Spiti Valley but it is frequently prepared and fondly eaten all over Himachal Pradesh.
2. **Alu Palda**: The potatoes are cooked in curd based gravy.
3. **Auriya Kaddoo or Kadoo Ka Khatta**: Khatta is indeed a very sumptuous dish made with pumpkin cooked in a spicy and tangy madra gravy and dried raw mango powder or amchoor along with other spices.
4. **Babru**: Babru is a famous dish of the Shimla. It has a filling of black daal along with spices. it is also called the bharwa puri and is served with vegetables and chutney. Babru is the Himachali version of kachoris.
5. **Balaaee:** It is a mildly spiced khichdi made with rice and kala chana cooked in butter milk with very few spices.
6. **Beduan Roti**: A very unique stuffed roti/paratha from the Kangra Valley region of Himachal Pradesh. This is a Makki roti stuffed with a spicy filling made with Arbi. The result is a filling and delicious paratha that needs just some buttermilk and white butter as accompaniment.
7. **Bhaturu**: Similar to Punjabi Bhatura
8. **Bhey or Spicy Lotus stems**: It is a delicious dish which is prepared with the lotus stems. Thinly sliced lotus stems are then cooked in the ginger-garlic, onions and gram flour which add the unique and great taste to the dish.
9. **Chha ghost**: This is a lamb dish, having it's origin in the Chamba district of Himachal Pradesh. This dish is prepared by marinating the lamb and then cooking it on a low flame. The gravy of this dish is made up of curd

and gram flour.

10. **Dhoe Dal**: Dhoe dal is a simple and delicious dal recipe prepared with urad dal. It is a popular dish in Himachal Pradesh, served with rice or roti.
11. **Madra**: Madra is a dish which belongs to the Chamba district of Himachal Pradesh. It is made using chickpeas, curd, coconut and different varieties of spices, which enhance the flavour of the dish.
12. **Marchu**: It is small sized sweet fermented bread. It is made from dough of wheat flour and semolina with milk, oil, yeast, fennel, dry fruits and Jaggery. the doudh is fermented, pressed and then deep fried.
13. **Mash Daal**: Mash daal or kali daal is made with split black lentils or ma ki daal. It is soaked overnight, pressure cooked and then simmered in a heavy bottomed pan along with thinly sliced onions, ginger, garlic and spices shallow fried in hot mustard oil to give the comforting mash daal.
14. **Mittha**: Mittha as the name suggests is a local dessert of Himachal Pradesh. It is prepared with sweetened rice mixed with a generous helping of raisins and other dry fruits.
15. **Pahadi Chicken**: A very simple dish, this is chunks of chicken which is stir- fried and cooked in a variety of flavours and spices. The Chicken is cooked with coriander, garlic and ginger along with mint and spices.
16. **Patande**: A popular breakfast dish of Sirmour district, Patande can rightly be called as Indian pancakes. Ladle full of smooth batter made from wheat flour, milk and sugar are poured on a ghee laden hot griddle and a thin pancakes like those resembling dosa(s) are made and cooked.
17. **Raintha:** A traditional raita made with Khajur, Palak, and Walnut paste.
18. **Sepu Vadi**: Sepu vadi is a delicious Himachali dish prepared by frying urad dal dumplings. It is a popular dish served during weddings and other special occasions.
19. **Siddu:** The siddu is one of the most famous Himachali dish from Shimla and Kullu . This dish is made by adding stuffing to the fermented dough and then it is steamed. The siddu is served with ghee, curd or chutney.
20. **Tawa Murgh**: Chicken pieces marinated in curd, cream and freshly ground garam masala topped with a sizzling tempering of red chillies and coriander.
21. **Tudikiya bath:** The Tudkiya bath is very famous in the district of Chamba. This rice is prepared by adding a takda to the rice along with spices, vegetables, curd, coriander etc. It is accompanied by chutney, curd and drops of lime juice to add a tangy flavour to the dish.

CHAPTER SEVENTEEN

Dhams and Community meals of Himachal Pradesh

Dhaam:

> "*Dham is a traditional festive feast of Himachal Pradesh prepared during religious festivals.*"

The origins of *Dham* are said to go back to Chamba Valley more than 1000 years ago. The Rajas ordered the cooks to make a meal that would justify as an offering for the Gods. The cooks prepared a variety of dishes from across the valleys and since then the tradition of Dham has continued in fairs, festivals, social functions and traditional community meal. *Dham* is a traditional festive meal, cooked only by *botis* (a particular caste of Brahmins who are hereditary chefs). The entire meal is *satwik*, which means even onion, ginger or garlic is not used to prepare it.

However, with time, dham was served on every occasion and gathering like marriages, family events and religious events in Himachal Pradesh. Preparations for this elaborate mid-day meal begin a night before. The temporary kitchen called *Rasialu* is usually built outside the main house with bamboo sticks as main pillars and steel sheets as roof. The entire food is cooked on wooden fire called *samdah* in 6 ×2 feet trench . The deep trench with fire is called *Char* or *Tuin*. Food is generally cooked in thick copper and brass vessels with broad base and narrow opening called *Charoti* or *Batloi* and everyone sits on the ground with cross legged in rows or */Bainth* to have food. It is served in courses on *pattals / Pattalu* or leaf plates (dried leaves of sal and banyan trees weaved together with thin pleats of bamboo sticks).

The most unique aspect of the dham is that no vegetables are used in any of the dishes (exception Kinnaur and Lahaul and spiti). It is purely made from various types of lentils and dairy products. The typical menu for a *dham* would start with rice and *madrah* of *rajma* (red kidney beans) cooked in yoghurt in Chamba, *sepubari* in Mandi district and mash dal in Kullu. This is followed by *kadi* and a *moong dal* (green lentil broth). The dal is made by smoked cooking method where mustard oil is put over a piece of burning coal and put in the dal. It is then covered for some time to get the smoky flavour- *Dhuni* technique. Topped by *khatta* (sweet and sour sauce made from tamarind and jaggary), the *dham* ends with the *mittha* (dessert) – sweet rice, liberally mixed with raisins and dry fruit.

The person responsible for filling water, cleaning, and washing utensils is called *Panihara*, and it is his duty to clean the *Painth* area after each batch finishes partaking food.

In Ayurveda, Ahar (food) is considered as one of a major tripod of life. As per Ayurveda a good diet consist of all six rasa and are taken in proper sequence of Madhura followed by Amla, Lavana, Katu, Tikta and Kashaya. Thus Dham is a good example of complete food as per Ayurveda having all six rasa and is served in proper sequence. The traditional Dham differs in every region of the state. However the Kangri Dham is the most famous among all, which comprises of almost 10 to 11 dishes. The dham ends with the mitha bhaat – sweet rice or *mithaee* (made of boondi or bread crumbs etc.). Dishes in a Kangri dham are devoid of artificial colours and are a perfect blend of oils and spices essential for the body.

The famous Dhams and their special cookery:

Chamba – Chambyali Dham- One of my most favourite of dhams across Himachal Pradesh, Chambyali dham can be said to be the birthplace of dham with regards to the history. The dishes are dominated by Madra and rajmah and kaala chana is a must. The madra dishes are oozing with ghee and are to be eaten with rice. Chamba kadhi is another dish of Chamba dham with gucchi (local mushroom) pulao. Khatta is also served with available vegetables and the dham is topped off with a sweet dish. It can be sweet pulao or even halwa mixed with poppy seeds.

Kangra – Kangri Dham- The Kangri Dham Thali's speciality is *telia mah*, black lentil dal doused in ghee and mixed lightly with spices; served with chickpeas madra, *kaale chane ka* khatta (sweet and sour black gram mahni) and other curries served with rice. Moong dal is also used in some dishes. Kangri dham also makes use of the *dhuni* technique wherein, mustard oil is poured over a piece of burning coal and is placed in the dish and covered for some time to give the smoky flavor that is called dhuni.

Mandi – Mandiyali Dham-They follow the Ayurvedic pattern of serving food where the sweet dish is served first. *Boondi ka meetha* (Bengal gram flour dipped in sweet syrup) denotes the starting of the meal in Mandyali dham. After that, the feast begins.

Sepuvadi (Fresh spinach leaves are made into a gravy and vadi is a deep fried fritter of black lentil and bengal gram) is served with rice. Next on the serving platter is *kaddu ka khatta* (Sweet and sour pumpkin dish made with tamarind and jaggery) and *mah ki dal* (black lentil dal) made in copious amounts of ghee. A different variety of *madra* with kidney beans is prepared and the ubiquitous *kadhi* is also served to be eaten with rice. Sometimes khatte chane (sweet and sour bengal gram) are also made and served in Mandiyali dham. The dham is finished by serving jhol – buttermilk like drink made by mixing curd and water.

Kullu – Kullvi Dham- Kullvi Dham doesn't have many different dishes as compared to Mandyali Dham but the serving process differs. Like Chambyali Dham, 2-3 different types of madra like rajmah madra, chickpea madra and *Gucchi Madra* are served first with rice. The dham continues with *telia maash* (oil fried black lentils) with delicious kadhi, chane ka khatta and meetha chawal (sweet rice) completes the feast.

Kinnauri Dham- In Kinnauri dham, rice is served along with puri, halwa, and seasonal vegetables. There is also provision of liquor and mutton for the guests. Apricot finds its way in different chutneys.

Hamirpuri dham-Traditional madra is the epic of this region prepared with pungent flavouring mustard oil. Onions and tomatoes are used wisely, but curd finds its place in many of the dishes. Dried apricots are used for preparing *khattas. Palda,* Maah dal rajmah and chana dal are the most sophisticated mouthwatering novelities.

Lahauli dham- In Lahaul and Spiti district, rice is served along with chana dal (Bengal gram), rajmah (kidney beans), chole (chick pea), aloo gobhi sabji, and mutton. Hot spicesand the use of ginger, garlic and onion is very common and in almost all the dishes.

Unaini dham- In Unaini dham , rice, *chana daal, rajmah, maah ki daal* along with *palda* finds a special place in *dham.* Almost all feasts culminate with Boondi kaa meetha. The Food, the style of preparation and the eating habits of the people of this district is very much influenced by Punjab and Chandigarh.

Solani dham- Dham served in Solan, use onion and tomatoe based gravy for preparing dishes. Raita with cuccumber and *Ramban* (a wild thorny tree branch) is used as digester. The *Dhungar* technique (adding smoky flavor) is used on Raita. Sooji ka halwa cooked in desi ghee is served as a sweet dish and usually served as the first course of Dham. Seasonal vegetables like Yam (Jimikund), Matar paneer, urad dal and a potato preparation is used in these areas.

Sirmauri dham- In Sirmouri dham, rice, maah ki daal, pude, jalebi, halwa, and shakkar are served in dham. Patande, ainkulu, and sidu are some of the famous foods of Sirmaur district.

Bilaspuri dham- In this moong dal cooked in ghee, serving as a rich source of carbohydrates; simple urad daal and tur daal cooked in the mouth-watering white mustard paste, followed by spicy sebu badi. Adding to the savory menu is *khatta*, which is unique as it consists of pumpkin, chickpeas, tamarind, and jaggery followed by the kadi pakoda which is a must. In the end, a sweet dish bundi ka meetha is served glazing the feast with irresistible kaleidoscopic colors.

Shimlai dham- In rural Shimla, maah ki daal, chane ki daal, safed chane kamadra, jimikand (yam), paneer, kale chane ka khatta, and sweets such as badana (Boondi) or small-sized gulab jamuns are served.

CHAPTER EIGHTEEN

Festivals and Fairs of Himachal Pradesh

The Fairs and Festivals of Himachal Pradesh have their own unique charm. Showcasing the rich cultural heritage of Himachal Pradesh the varieties of fairs and festivals of the state are worth participating. During the festive season, the people of Himachal Pradesh wear colourful dresses and adorn themselves with elegant jewellery. This is also the time when the people make a variety of mouth-watering traditional dishes. Dance and music are also a part of the celebrations. Different regions have their own dance forms, but folk music is popular among all the Himachalis. The popular dance forms of the state are the Rakshasa dance, the Kayang dance, the Bakayang dance, Rasa dance and the Jhoor dance.

Some of the fairs and festivals celebrated in Himachal Pradesh are:

- **Halda festival** – Welcome the New Year - Halda Festival Himachal Pradesh Dedicated to the goddess of wealth, Shashikar Apa, Halda festival is celebrated with great zeal and enthusiasm in order to celebrate the new year. The actual date of the celebration is decided by the Lamas. People of Lahaul districts come together and enjoy their new year by performing music.
- **Lohri /Maghi** - Lohri Festival Himachal Pradesh Lohri is a feisty festival celebrated by the people of Himachal Pradesh, Haryana and Punjab. In the villages of Punjab, Lohri is celebrated as a ceremonial ritual to jumpstart the harvesting of Rabi crop.

- **Losar Festival** - Losar Festival Himachal Pradesh The New Year celebration of Tibetans, Losar festivals takes place in the first week of the first lunar month (February), with performances of Tibetan opera and prayer ceremonies being held at various monasteries.
- **Doongri Festival, Kullu** - Doongri Festival Himachal Pradesh Doongri festival or Hadimba Devi fair is celebrated in Kullu in honor of and to celebrate Hadimba Devi's (wife of Bhima) birthday. A huge fair is organized on this day; during the festival one can catch glimpses of dance and musical performances by local artists.
- **Maha Shivaratri** - Maha Shivaratri Himachal Pradesh Maha Shivratri is celebrated in the month of February with great zeal and enthusiasm. Shivratri was the day when Lord Shiva married Goddess Parvati. Maha Shivaratri literally means _The Night of Shiva.'
- **Nalwari Fair** - Nalwari Fair Himachal Pradesh Celebrated with great pomp and show since colonial times, Nalwari fair is a great platform for all the cattle traders to meet and do business.
- **Baisakh/** Vaisakhi - Baisakh or Vaisakhi is marked as the end of the winter season as per the agrarian tradition.
- **Rakhidumni** (Rakhi) Festival - Rakhidumni or Rakhi is celebrated on the full moon day in the monsoon month of Bhadrapad. The festival is celebrated to acknowledge the emotional bond of brother and sister.
- **Phulaich Festival** - Phulaich Festival Himachal Pradesh Phulaich means _the festival of flowers' and as per Hindu calendar it is organized in the month of Bhadrapada. The festival is associated with the blooming of flowers in the Kinnaur valley.
- **Chet Festival** - (Dholru) is the first month of the lunar year and the first day of the month is cellebrated with a belief to bring hapiness and prosperity.

CHAPTER NINETEEN

Classical Recipes from the Himachali Kitchens

1. Besan Ki Sabzi

(This dish is prepared in most of the states in the North, with local variations. A very good substitute for vegetables in their off seasons).

Ingredients:

- 250g Besan (gram flour),
- 100g Curd, 1 tsp Haldi (turmeric),
- 1 tsp Ajwain,
- 1 pinch Hing (asafoetida),
- 1 No Capsicum medium,
- ½ sprig Coriander leaves,
- 1 inch Ginger chopped,
- 2 No Green Chillies chopped,
- 1 tsp Saunf (fennel),
- Salt to taste.

For Gravy:

- 250g Curd,
- 1 Tbsp Garam Masala,
- 2 Tbsp Besan,
- 1 tsp red chilli powder,
- 1 tsp turmeric powder,
- 150g Onion, 150gTomatoes,

- 1 Tbsp Dry mango powder (amchur),
- 2 tsp Coriander powder,
- 100 ml Oil,
- Salt to taste.

Method:
Gravy:

- Heat oil, add garam masala.
- Sauté onions, add tomatoes, and cook till tomatoes are tender.
- Make a mixture of besan, curd, water and the remaining ingredients, in a separate bowl.
- Add this mixture to the pan. Get to boil once then strain the gravy.
- Cook again till it boils once and let it simmer for 15 minutes.
- The gravy is ready to be used.

Sabzi:

- Mix besan, curd and turmeric.
- Strain and cook the mixture with all the remaining ingredients, except coriander leaves.
- Cook till it achieves a thick consistency.
- Cool it in a platter. Cut into small cubes.
- Add these cubes to the gravy.
- Garnish with coriander leaves. Serve hot.

2. *Ankley*

(Rice Pancakes)
Ingredients:

- 3 cups Rice flour
- Water as needed
- Salt

Method:

- Combine the ingredients in a bowl to make a smooth batter.
- Heat a tawa and apply ghee on it.
- Pour a ladle of batter on the tawa and spread it evenly.
- Cook the pancakes on both sides.
- Serve Ankley hot with dal.

3. Redu

(Redu is a popular Himachali dish made with curd and green garlic. It tastes great with makki roti.)

Ingredients:

- 1 medium bowl Curd/Dahi
- 1 -2 stems Green garlic, chopped
- Green chilli , chopped
- Jeera
- Red chilli powder
- Turmeric powder
- Dry coriander
- Hing (dissolved in water)
- Salt to taste

Method:

- Heat a tbsp. ghee in a pan and add jeera, coriander and green garlic. Sauté for a minute.
- Add red chilli powder, turmeric, hing water and salt to taste. Cook for another minute.
- Switch off the stove and add beaten curd. Mix well.
- Serve Redu with makki roti.

4. Kathal madra

(Kathal madra is a delicious Himachali recipe where jackfruit is cooked in a yogurt gravy. You can serve this dish with rice or bread.)

Ingredients:

- 500 grams Jackfruit, cut into 1 or 2 inch pieces
- 200 grams Yogurt
- 1/2 teaspoon Turmeric
- 1/2 tablespoon Coriander powder
- 1 Cardamom, big
- 2 Cardamom, small
- 12 Kalamirch
- 1 Cinnamon, inch long
- 2 Cloves
- 2 Bay Leaf
- Cumin seeds
- 1 pinch Asafetida
- Ghee
- Fresh Coriander Leaves
- Salt to taste

Method:

- Pressure cook jackfruit with salt and water for 2 or 3 whistles.
- Heat oil. Fry large cardamom, small cardamom, black pepper, cinnamon, bay leaves and cloves. Heat for a while and grind it.
- Heat ghee. Splutter cumin seeds and asafoetida. Add ground spices. Roast for a minute.
- Add jackfruit, turmeric, coriander powder, and red pepper powder and mix well.
- Add yogurt and mix well. Cook on a low flame until it boil.
- Add salt and fresh coriander leaves. Serve Kathal madra hot with rice or bread.

5. Khus Khus Ka Halwa

(Khus khus ka halwa is a delicious dessert made with poppy seeds. It is a very nutritious and healthy dish that is really easy to make).

Ingredients:

- 1/4 cup Poppy seeds, soaked overnight
- 1 cup Milk
- 3/4 cup Sugar
- 1/2 teaspoon Dry coconut
- 1/4 cup Ghee
- Dry fruits for garnish
- A pinch of cardamom powder

Method:

- Grind poppy seeds to a fine paste by adding little milk.
- Heat ghee in a pan and add poppy seed paste. Stir constantly.
- Cook until the paste turns light brown in color.
- Add rest of the milk and keep stirring until all the moisture evaporates.
- Add coconut and cardamom powder. Mix well.
- Garnished khus khus ka halwa with dry friuts and serve.

Part C: UTTARAKHAND (KUMAON AND GARHWAL)

Kumaon (Western Part) and Garhwal (Eastern Part)

CHAPTER TWENTY

Geography of Uttarakhand

Uttarakhand, located at the foothills of Shivalik range of the Great Himalayas of Northern India is formed from north western districts of Uttar Pradesh. It borders Nepal on the east, Tibet on the north, Himachal Pradesh on the west, Uttar Pradesh on the south and Haryana in the northwest.

> *"Uttarakhand can be divided into several physiographic zones, all running parallel to each other from northwest to southeast. The northern zone, popularly known as the Himadri, contains segments of the Zaskar and the Great Himalaya ranges. Adjacent to and south of the Great Himalayas is a zone containing the Lesser Himalayas known popularly as the Himachal. To the south of the Himachal is a stretch of the Siwalik Range. The entire area containing the Himadri, the Himachal, and the Siwaliks is broadly known as the Kumaun Himalayas."*

The southern edge of the Siwalik Range merges with a narrow bed of gravel and alluvium known as the *Bhabar*, which interfaces to the southeast with the marshy terrain known as the *Tarai*. South of the Siwaliks are found flat-floored depressions, known locally as duns, such as the Dehra Dun.The state is divided naturally by Nanda Devi Mountains in two regions, the western half known as *Garhwal* and the eastern region as *Kumaon*.

Dehradun, the capital, is the railhead and the largest city of the state. Nainital is where the high court of Uttarakhand is located. Both Kumaon and Garhwal have beautiful natural scenario, with a series of imposing mountain peaks of *Chowkhamba, Bhagirathi, Pindari, Nanda Devi, Sahastrataal, Kedarnath, Gangotri, Milam, Jogin* to name a few. Nanda Devi, having an altitude of 25,643 feet is the highest mountain in Uttarakhand.

Out of a total area of 53483 km^2, the state of Uttarakhand is 65%covered by forest and 86% is mountainous. Two of India's mightiest rivers, the Ganges and the Yamuna start off from the glaciers of Uttarakhand. The *Valley of Flowers*, a world heritage site designated by UNESCO, well known for the all absorbing beauty and variety of the rare plants and flowers, is located near Joshimath in Garhwal.The presence of several hill stations, wildlife parks, pilgrimage places and trekking routes make Uttarakhand an attractive tourist destination.

CHAPTER TWENTY-ONE

History of Uttarakhand

> "*Archaeological evidence like ancient rock paintings, paleoloithic stone tools, rock shelters, megaliths, etc suggest that this mountainous state had been frequented and inhabited from prehistoric times.*"

Findings in Chamoli and Almorah districts clearly reveal the existence of human habitation from Stone Age in this state. The name of this state can be found in the great Purans and Vedas and the legendary epic of Ramayana and Mahabharata.

During Vedic age, Uttarakhand formed a part of Panchal and Kuru kingdom (*mahajanpads*). In Hindu mythology also, Uttarakhand has been recognized as a part of the famed *Kedarkhand* (now Garhwal) and *Manaskhand* (Kumaon). Kunindas were the first major dynasties of Kumaon during 2nd century BC. According to findings, Kunindas practiced an early form of Shaivism. Early presence of Buddhism has been noted in Kalsi region where Ashokan edicts have been found. The kingdoms of Kumaon and Garhwal, were formed during the medieval period. The region fell to the Gorkha empire of Nepal in 1803, but in 1816, British took over the kingdom after winning the Anglo-Nepalese war, and formed the Treaty of Sugauli.

Garhwal Kingdom: Founded in the year 888 AD this kingdom later on became a part of the British raj in India. People from this region were active participants in the quit India movement which was waged against the British. Later on, while on one side Sardar Vallabhbhai Patel was working towards the unification of India on the other end, the people of Garhwal themselves were forcing the king to accept the concept of a sovereign India. In 1949 the last ruler of Garhwal – Manavendra Shah gave up and Garhwal officially became a part of India.

Kumaon Region: Meanwhile the Kumaon region of Uttarakhand was a complete battle field. Before the British annexation 8 princely states existed in the regions that were in complete control. The eastern Garhwal was attached with the newly annexed Kumaon region. Just like the Garhwal population, Kumaon people also actively participated in the quit India movements along with being heavily influenced by the teachings and motivation by Mahatma Gandhi. This is the reason why the people here immediately and very willingly India's sovereignty.

The word Uttarakhand literally translates into "*North part of the Land*" and it was formerly a part of Uttar Pradesh and was known as Uttaranchal then.

The similarity of traditions, geography, and proximity to different ethnic groups brought Kumaon and Garhwal closer forgetting their long rivalry, and this had greatly strengthened the movement for statehood of Uttarakhand in 1990. Finally, on 9th November 2000, the birth of Uttarakhand took place by carving out 13 districts from Uttar Pradesh. It became the 27th state of India with Dehradun as its capital. The name Uttarakhand was coined for the state, which was changed later as Uttaranchal and again it was renamed as Uttarakhand.

This state is also referred to as *Devbhoomi* or the land of gods and goddesses due to the presence of some of the most ancient temples, shrines and pilgrimages.

CHAPTER TWENTY-TWO

Climate & Agriculture of Uttarakhand

Climate of Uttarakhand:

Uttarakhand mainly has two different climatic regions, namely, the hilly terrain and the smaller plain region. So, the weather is also quite varied, depending on the particular place. Summers in the plain region of Uttarakhand have similar climate as other surrounding plain regions of different states i.e the maximum temperature can cross the 40°C mark and there can be considerable humidity. Warm temperate conditions prevail in the Middle Himalayan valleys with temperature around 25°C making it an idle getaway for people of the plains to beat the heat. However, in the higher areas of middle Himalayas the temperature is around 15 to 18°C, still pleasant. The season extends from April to June.

The Climate of Uttarakhand during winters in the plain region can be chilly with temperatures going below 5°C mark. The winters in the middle Himalayan valleys are very cold and in the higher areas the temperature can drop below the freezing point. The Himalayan peaks remain snowcapped throughout the year and many places receive regular snowfall. Throughout the state the temperature ranges from sub-zero to 15°C and the season lasts from November to February.The monsoon is the most pleasant season when temperature differs from 15 to 25°C at most places which reigns from July to September. The state receives 90% of its annual rainfall in this season.

The eastern parts of Himalayas are subjected to heavier rainfalls when westerns are relatively drier.

Agriculture and the Staple Food of the Uttarakhandi:

Agricultural practices are the main stay of the people of Uttarakhand. Out of the total population, more than 75% people are engaged either with the main occupation of agriculture or its allied practices, dominated by traditional subsistence cereal farming. Agricultural crops are grown almost in all the altitudinal zones — from the low-lying areas, which are called "*Gangarh or Bhangar*", to the highly elevated region, where the legendary term is given as "*Danda*".

Farming is done by three methods:

1. **Contour farming**- is growing crops *"on the level"* across or perpendicular to a slope rather than up and down the slope. The rows running across the slope are designed to be as level as possible to facilitate tillage and planting operations on the contour as well as prevent soil erosion and retention of moisture.
2. **Terrace farming**- when the land is quite sloppy, then 'steps' known as terraces are built. This type of land retains the water, stops soil erosion and loss of nutrients.
3. **Jhoom Farming** is basically adopted by the nomads. They clear a certain area of the forest and start cultivation there. After few years when the soil becomes unusable or loses its fertility, they leave the place in search of another suitable forest land.

The growing of crops varies according to the heights. Among them, the main crops are rice, wheat, millet, barley, all types of pulses, all types of oilseeds and almost all types of fruits. The crops, vegetables and fruits of all varieties are grown in the different climatic zones such as tropical, temperate, and cold because, the region is characterized by the different altitudinal zones elevated from 200 meters to more than 8000 meters. As a result, different climates are found from hot tropical to sub temperate and chilly cold. Pulses varieties are grown extensively.

Among vegetables, potato, onion, carrot, all types of green leafy vegetables, brinjal, pumpkin, ladyfinger, pea, gram, radish, ginger, garlic, etc, are grown widely. All fruit varieties are grown in the different altitudinal zones.

The main fruits are Peach (*Aadoo*), Plum (*Pulam*), Apricot (*Khumanee*), Pears (*Nashpati*), Cherry, Mango, Mekauti (*Malta*), Litchi, *Dadim*, Guava,

Jackfruit, Apple, Strawberry, Lemon, *Chakotra* (Grape Fruit), *Narangi* (Orange), *Kirmodi* or *Kirmoli, Hisaaloo* or *Aisayloo, Kafal* (Bayberry), *Ghigharu, Alu Bukhara* (Plum), Timil, *Fantullo, Bhayanbhalo, TingloPhalalo* Pine Nuts and *Bedu*, while the juices preferred are Buransh (rhododendron) juice, rose juice and malta juice.

In spite of feasible climatic conditions, agricultural dominant society, and availability of all types of crops, the production and productivity of these crops are very low, even they are unable to meet the grain-need of the people in Uttarakhand. Like most of India, agriculture is one of the most significant sectors of the economy of Uttarakhand.

Agricultural export zones have been set up in the state for leechi, horticulture, herbs, medicinal plants, and basmati rice. The people living in higher villages are deprived of fresh vegetables and fruit and also wheat or rice. They generally grow grain such as *mandua* and barley which becomes their staple food.

The Bhotia tribes are nomadic and are engaged in moslty agriculture and trade. Ingredients exported were food grain, sugar, gur (jaggery), spices, tobacco, cotton, cloths, corals, beads etc. and items imported were borax, salt and wool. They cultivate cultivate grains like Mandua or palti (buckwheat), phaphar, naphal (hill wheat), paddy, maize, jowar, potato etc. As the Bhotia community is seasonally nomadic, storing dehydrated or sun-dried food for the winter is a common practice. They dry vegetables like onion, radish, herbs, spices and meat. "*Lafhoo*" is a popular preparation of radish, made by grating and then sun-drying it. The sun-dried grated radish is then prepared into a stew (*jholi*) and served with rice. *Thawe* (caraway seeds) is commonly used in dal and chilli chutney.

Mountain herbs are widly used in their food. *Kwacho* (Sakwa), another wild herb, is also used in dal and with fried vegetables. *Chibi* is prepared with rajma dal, *Timor* is a herb, used in chutney with chillies. Roti and *Dulang* (sacred bread- offered to God) is made from the different kinds of wheat available and also with *Kutu* or Kodo*Guthain* (pancake) and *Jadu* (porridge) made from wheat is a part of their everyday diet. Wild Goat, also called "*Phasi*", is a popular dish of the community.

Different parts of Phasi are dried in the sun and smoked after marinating the meat in salt. The dried meat is preserved and carried to the lower settlements for winter. "*Jaama*", dried intestine of the wild goat, is also preserved and used in many preparations. Apart from Phasi, Bhotias eat goat, wild boar and wild chicken.

CHAPTER TWENTY-THREE

Culture and Traditions of Uttarakhand

Uttarakhand is also known as *"Dev Bhoomi"* the land of the gods and religion and spirituality exists in the soul of every Pahari and can be visible in their daily life. Large segment of the people in Uttarakhand, especially in the upper reaches, are orthodox Buddhists and Hindus. Many of Hinduism's most important shrines like

Char Dham of Uttarakhand:

"Char Dham" - the four shrines of **Gangotri, Yamunotri, Badrinath and Kedarnath**, (a pilgrimage of which is supposed to ensure instant salvation) lie tucked in the mountains and along the rivers of the state. The sacred Ganga, on its foaming path down to the plains, meets its tributaries at what are called the **Panch Prayag**- the five sacred `sangams" of the river at Vishnuprayag, Nandprayag, Karnaprayag, Rudraprayag and Devprayag.

And that is not all; **Hardwar and Rishikesh** are two of Hinduism's most prominent destinations for pilgrims, while the historical **Gurudwara of Hemkund Sahib**, near the Valley of Flowers, is an important shrine for Sikh. The **Kumbh Mela** that is held every twelve years witnesses some of the largest gatherings of devotees to be seen anywhere in the whole world. Overwhelming natural panoramas accompany the pilgrims taking part in the Nanda Devi Raj Jaat and Kailash Mansarovar Yatras.

Similarly the Dargaah at Piran Kaliyar Sharif, holds a significant religious rank for Muslims and people from other faiths alike.

According to a 2007 study, Uttarakhand has the highest percentage of Brahmins of any state in India, with approximately 20% of the population being Brahmin. Muslims, Sikhs, Christians, Buddhists, and Jains make up the remaining population with the Muslims being the largest minority.

> "*The culture of the people of Uttarakhand is enriched by features like its music and dance, festivals, cuisine, arts and crafts. All the local traditions of the state are determinedly attached to nature and its bounty.*"

No legends or myths are complete without nature, seasons or the Himalayas being integral part of them. The people spare no opportunity to celebrate this bountiful natural, social and religious diversity. Collective celebrations become the order of the day – the many fairs and festivals bear testimony to this. These fairs have now become remarkable stages for all sort of uncluttered social, cultural and economic exchange.

The religious bonds between the people is held tight by features like music, dance and arts and thus the people are in turn deep -rooted in their religion with awe inspiring Himalayas.

The people of Uttarakhand never miss out on any celebration of festivals for they take the slightest possible opportunity to celebrate all the festivals of India with great enthusiasm. Some of the national festivals celebrated by them include Holi, Diwali, Navratri, Christmas and Durgotsav. The people here generally get very excited about festivals and they take an active participation in it by fasting, joining the festival processions, cooking food, etc.

Some of the festivals pertaining to the people of Uttarakhand during which their distinct customs and traditions are followed includes *Basant Panchami, Bhitauli, Harela, Phooldei, Batsavitri, Ganga Dusshera, Dikar Puja, Olgi or Ghee Sankranti, Khatarua, Ghuian Ekadashi and Ghughutia.*

At the time of monsoon and on the first day of the month of `Shravana` a Kumaoni festival known as *Harela* is celebrated with great pomp and religious fervor.

The love between a brother and a sister is shared by exchanging of gifts between them on the festival of *Bhitauli* and this is celebrated in the month of Chaitra. They follow age old customs and traditions for all social functions like new birth, marriage, death, etc.

The Bhotia tribes, who are somewhat related to Tibetan people are mostly located in the upper regions of Pithoragargh district. They are mostly mountain dwellers engaged in agriculture and trade. The offer a special type of designed roti called *Dulung*to their gods. They celebrate the *Losar* festival during the flowering of the apricot trees in autumn and *Kandali* festival in the rainy season. Several indigenous tribes and communities flourish in this state today maintaining their distinct cultural heritage and traditions. The several fairs and festivals celebrated by the tribes such as *Bhotias* (Shaukas), *Tharus*, *Buxas* and *Jaunsaris* are opportune for the locals and the visitors to witness these events as opportunities to keep the traditional modes of life and art alive apart from providing them the recognition they so strongly deserve.

> "*Legends, myths and anecdotes galore in the state of Uttarakhand which has in turn been bestowed by the richest, holy rivers and the most esteemed mountains. Series of legends and tales are intricately woven around the sacred shrines, temples and rivers by simple hearted, god-fearing people that simultaneously reflect the socio-cultural diversity of the state.*"

CHAPTER TWENTY-FOUR

Important Features of the Uttarakhandi Cookery

Characteristically grain and cereal based, made up of simple ingredients, cooked with minimal spicing, simple temperings and optimal cooking methods into flavourful, filling and nutritious meals. "*Ghar ka khana*" or made at home, is a very important phenomenon for Uttarakhandis. Most of the food is steamed, boiled, roasted or baked. The food of every Pahari is incomplete without dal, chutney and a sweet dish. In the kitchens of Kumaon, a wide range of pulses is used to create mouth-watering recipes, which are usually enjoyed with rice.

> "*The pulses, beverages, and fruits here are quite different from other parts of India.*"

The distinct flavours of Pahari food are prominent in the cuisine with the use of mustard and cumin seeds not only adding a distinct taste but also acting as appetizers.

Though the people in the higher mountainous regions use generic spices and herbs found in most Indian homes, they also use some very indigenous ingredients like *Pahadimirch* (which are spicy enough to get one's ears smoking) and *bhaang* (Hemp) pods, which grow in the wilderness, *Faran* (similar to onion family) is a super tasty spice which can be used in a host of Indian dishes including dal and vegetables. Tiny dark mustard like spice called *Jakhiya* (small black seeds which grow wild and are often used in tempering, the way we use mustard or cumin seeds), *Gandreni* (a dried root which is used in place of asafoetida), yellow chillies and *Jambu* (wild herbs that are dried and used like we use kasuri methi).

In the monsoons, they have virtually a treasure trove of wild greens like fiddlehead ferns called *Lingur, Lai* (a close cousin of red mustard) and plenty of *Sisunag* or*Bicchooghaas* or *Kandali* (stinging nettle) and *Lingadusaag* or *Lengda* (wild asparagus). Aerial yams called *Gethi* and *Chippi* (button mushroom) which proved to be an excellent ingredient for salads and soups. The use of tomato in the cuisine is minimal and food is essentially cooked in mustard oil or pure ghee and even the chutneys, namely *Bhang-jeera chutney*, are made using Bhang seeds.

Pahari meals are healthy, with a balanced use of fats; ghee to temper lentils, mustard oil for greens and vegetable oil for other dishes. Spices used are minimal. Garlic, ginger, chillies, asafeotida are favoured. The Pahadi communities get their proteins from river fish, mutton and robust dals are made with legumes like *Bhatt* (a black pulse), *Gahat* or *Gauth* or *Kulath* (horsegram), *Rajma, Toor, Masoor, Mung, Chana, Swanta* and *Gauthare and ras (*a mixture of dals). Lentils and pulses are also used to make unique local preparations like *Chainsoo*, a deliciously textured thick smoky gravy of roasted dal *Bhatwani* (a variety of soyabean) and *Phanu* (made with roughly ground Gahat soaked overnight and then boiled on slow fire for a long time), a textured aromatic gravy made from soaked crushed dal.

Urad dal is extremely important to Pahadi culinary culture and *Urad ki pakodi* (lentil fritters) and *Swala* (fried bread stuffed with potato) are ubiquitous to all celebratory occasions.

One of the traditional dishes that you can find in small eateries along the winding hill roads is *Aloo ke gutke*, which is essentially potato wedges fried with local herbs like *jakhya* and *jamboo* and then topped with coriander leaves.

During the warm summer months, the cooling *triphala* is included in the diet, while the monsoon sees the preparation of the delicious, warming *Surka*, a drink made with *Takeera* (soaked, pounded and dried wheat), almonds and cardamom. Hill spinach is a common dish to accompany chapatis made of *madua* or finger millet seeds. Topped with dollops of ghee and jaggery, this is an ideal winter dish.

Bhang too is used extensively to make chutneys. Its seeds are also used to make *Sana hua nimbu* from curd, radish, lemon and spices. Despite the high altitude and cold climatic conditions, they hardly use any oil. Every household owns cattle, so food is cooked mostly in clarified butter (*ghee*). In the rare event that oil is used, it is mustard oil.

The *Koda roti* is best served with *Kandali* (nettle leaves) *ka saag*and*lingadi (*fiddlehead fern)*kasaag*. The people in the Kumaon region relish large dried balls of urad dal, called *Badis*, and their smaller version prepared from Moong dal called *Mangodi*. These items help people in combating severe winter cold conditions. The Garhwali breakfast begins with *Mandua ki roti* (chapati made finger millet or ragi or nachni) or *Bhari roti* (chapati stuffed with cooked pulses, namely Gahat) or *Gahat ke paranthe*. Various other rotis are also eaten like *Marchhra roti* (made of chawlai seeds), *Bajra roti* and A*loo ke parathe*. *Kodo*, a coarse grain with high fiber content, has always been the energy diet of the people of the hill region.

Vegetables play an important part in Pahadi meals in the form of raitas, chutneys and subzis. Some may simply be tempered with jakhiya and chilies in mustard oil. Others cooked into simple gravy preparations called *jhols*. Lauki (white gourd), tori (ridge gourd), leafy greens like chawlai (amaranth), kaddu (green pumpkin), tukkulu and other regular vegetables are eaten in summer.

The monsoon brings colocassia leaves made into delicious *Patyud* (the Garhwali version of the patod/patra). Winter brings leafy greens like methi (fenugreek leaves), mooli ke patte (radish leaves), rai (mustard greens), and more. Pahadi palak (local spinach) is a particular favourite in the winter and is cooked into subzi and signature dishes like *kafuli*, a gravy thickened with rice or chickpea flour and *Dhabadi* made with arhar dal. *Thichwani* is a popular vegetable preparation made of pahadi mooli (round white raddish) that is "thinchaoed" or bashed up and cooked into delicious gravy.

As it might appear Pahadi cuisine is largely vegetarian but non-vegetarian dishes are much loved too although elaborate recipes are limited. River fish especially trout is fried or cooked into jhols (curries), an occasional chicken curry is eaten but meat- bhaat (mutton curry and rice) are still the most loved favourite. Meat came from hunting and when an animal was killed the whole carcass was put to use. Choice cuts cooked into curry, excess pickled, trotters made into *Dauni* soup, and intestines into *Bhuttua* (Cooked intestines, heart and liver of goat). One notable, traditional meat recipe is *Kachmauli* in which a goat is spit roasted, the meat is taken off the bone, tossed with mustard oil, salt, chili and turmeric and served.

Yoghurt is used a lot, especially in making the mouthwatering *Kheere ka raita* .

Food preservation is a regular part of the culinary calendar and there is a fantastic repertoire of options to zing up meals, from chutneys like *Chullu* and bhaang to til, pickles like kathal, kachner and flavoured salts like *Lehsun ka namak* (green garlic pounded with salt) to name a few.

The cuisine has something in store for those with a sweet tooth as well. Festivals and other occasions feature special foods like *Gujiyas* for Holi, Diwali starts with *Kheel patasha. Duseraa, Bhaiduj* and Weddings call for *Balushai, Chenamurkhi, Rabri malpua*, and piles and piles of *Roat* and *Aarsa. Bal mithai* is chocolate (milk reduced to solid form) studded with sugar balls can be found in sweet shops across the region. *Singhori* is a sweetmeat moulded in an indigenous leaf called *Malla ka patta* that results in little cones fragrant with an elusive scent of the leaf packaging. Another sweet tooth of the region includes the Kumaoni Puas. What makes Arsa different from the common malpua is the use of jaggary and curd in it. These melt-in-the mouth sweet balls can be munched on during tea time or as a dessert after meals. Jowar-like grain called *Jhangora* is popularly used to make kheer. *Rotana* (Sweet flour dumplings) is a traditional Garhwali sweet. No celebration of Uttarakhand is complete without it. *Singal* a traditional sweet snack usually made for weddings and other occasions.

> "*Bhotiyas relish on "Champaa", a roti made of barely roasted flour or boiled potatoes, rice or avegetable stew called "Thukpa". They drink Chakti and Jaan (local beer) that contains very low concentration of ethyl alcohol; Daru is distilled liquour that contains higher concentration of ethyl alcohol in all their celebrations.*"

CHAPTER TWENTY-FIVE

Cooking equipments and utensils used in Uttarakhand

1. Donga: Assorted serving bowl
2. Gol karchul: Ball Scoop
3. Katora: Big bowl
4. Botal: Bottle
5. Balti: Bucket
6. Plain Chaku: Butter knife
7. Katordaan: Chapati box
8. Dibba: Container
9. Pyala: Cup
10. Bhagona: Deep cylindrical vessel
11. Parat: Edged big plate
12. Thali: Edged small plate
13. Chhapta karchul: Flat spoon
14. Kanta: Fork
15. Keep: Funnel
16. Gas tandoor: Gas Oven
17. Chulha: Gas stove
18. Gilas: Glass
19. Kaddukas: Grater
20. Tawa: Griddle
21. Idli khancha: Idli mould
22. Martban: Jar
23. Jug: Jug
24. Chaku: Knife
25. Karchul: Ladle

26. Dhakkan: Lid
27. Machis: Matchbox
28. Okhli: Mortar
29. Degchi: Pan
30. Cheelne wala chaku/chheelar: Peeler
31. Lamba ched wala karchul: Perforated flat spoon
32. Gol Ched wala karchul /Jhara: Perforated spoon
33. Thali: Plate
34. Cheemta: Pliers
35. Cooker: Pressure cooker
36. Chakla: Rolling board
37. Belan: Rolling pin
38. Lota: Round water pot
39. Saucepan: Saucepan
40. Kainchi: lScissor
41. Katori: Serving bowl
42. Chota Karchul: Serving spoon
43. Chammach: Spoons
44. Bada chammach: Tablespoon
45. Chota Chammach: Teaspoon
46. Channi: Teastrainer
47. Sandsi/ Pakad: Tongs
48. Tray: Tray
49. Kadahi: Wok
50. Lakdi karchul: Wooden Spatula

CHAPTER TWENTY-SIX

Festival Cookery of Uttarakhand

1. **Aloo Daal Pakora**: Mashed potatoes are shaped into balls and dipped into a dal batter and deep fried. It is served as a snack and is one of the favorite snacks of the locality of the Kumaon. It is served with chutney or tomato ketchup. It is an innovative food of Kumaon.
2. **Aloo ke Gutke**: These are small pieces boiled potatoes cooked in spiced masalas and relished with cucumber raita, locally used as snacks in Kumaun region.
3. **Aloo Tamatar Jhol**: Pahari aloo cooked in spiced tomato thin gravy.
4. **Arsa:** A special Garhwali sweet dish. It is prepared on special occasion like marriages and festivals. It is prepared with jaggary, rice and mustard oil.
5. **Baadi:** Made of Kwado /Choon/Mandua flour cooked in small quantity of water to soft dough consistency and eaten with Gahat ki dal or Phaanu- a Garhwali preparation.
6. **Badil**: These are small cakes made from boiled and mashed pulses. The pulses are boiled with spices, ground, made into small cakes, fried and served. Kumaoun especiality.
7. **Bal Mithai**: These are brown chocolate-like fudge made with roasted khoya, coated with white sugar balls, and is a popular sweet from Almora.
8. **Bhang ki Chutney**: Roasted Bhang seeds (Hemp Seeds), cumin seeds and *darim* (a local variety of pomegranate) and mixed with lemon juice.
9. **Bhatt ki chutney**: roasted Bhatt dal , ground together with lemon, green chilli, green coriander to form a mouthwatering Garhwali chutney.
10. **Bhatwani Dal**: A delicious dal made from Bhatt.

11. **Bhumla**: Roasted whole green chana with its covering. Used as snacks
12. **Chainsoo**: It is made by roasted grain of Moong Dal and black Bhat. This Dal is very nutritious but hard to digest.
13. **Chanchyya**: It is type of light salted kadhi made from the starch of strained rice mixed with buttermilk.
14. **Palyo**: This is a type of thin kadhi made with jhangora or saawan rice or besan mixed with butter milk. This may be salted or sweet in taste.
15. **Chholyaan rota**: This dish is often eaten for breakfast or as a snack and has a pancake-like consistency. The batter is made of wheat flour with sugar or jaggery and fennel, which is then poured on a hot griddle and cooked on both sides till golden brown
16. **Dhabadi**: It is an palak arhar dal from Garahwal.
17. **Dubuk**: It is a dal prepared by coarsely ground Gahat or bhatt.
18. **Dwancha or timur chutney**: This is a chutney prepared by the Bhotias using Timur and tomatoes.
19. **Phanu**: Phanu is also made of dals (lentils) like chainsoo, but in this case the dals are soaked in water for about 4 to 6 hours before its use. A different variety of dals like- Gahat, Arhar or green Mung can be used to prepare Phanu.
20. **Ghughuti:** is fried sweet preparations of various shapes and sizes prepared by each Kumauni household during the festival of maker sankranti. These sweets are then tied into a string and are garlanded around the children's neck in order to attract birds (especially crows). Wheat Flour, Dry Fruits, Sauf (Fennel Seeds), Sesame Seeds, Grated Dry Coconut, Sooji (for crunchiness), Ghee (for softness), Jaggery Syrup (as per dish quantity), Milk are kneaded together to form the soft dough.
21. **Gahat dal** (Kulath): horse gram dal also known as gahat, muthira, kulath, or kulthi is widely eaten in Uttarakhand. It is a good source of iron and is very beneficial in stomach, blood and kidney related disease.
22. **Gahat Soup**: It is soup made from Gahat (Kulth) Grains.
23. **Gidkiyu**: This is a types of soup made from mandwa ata.
24. **Gulgula**: These are sweet Fritters (mitha pakora) made either refined flour or a mixture of ripe banana and refined flour. A festival dish.
25. **Jhangore ki Kheer**: Sweet dish prepared with Jhangora
26. **Jhol**: It is a very light gravy made of tomatoes, potatoes and other tubers.
27. **Jholi**: It is thick gravy made of various pulses, Phannu like preparation.
28. **Jya**: A type of salted tea.

29. **Kachmauli**: Goat is spit roasted; the meat is taken off the bone, tossed with mustard oil, salt, chili and turmeric and served.
30. **Kapa**: A curry dish made by minced spinach and mustard leaves.
31. **Kurunthi**: Urad dal pakore.
32. **Mooli ki thinchodi**: This dish derives its name from the method of its preparation. Pahari mooli (mountain radish) and potatoes are pounded (not cut) with the help of a small pestle called sil-batta. These are then cooked in mustard oil in a kadhai with Jakhya and tomato paste
33. **Kafuli:** It is a thick gravy Daal made of green leafy vegetables (preferably radish leaves) and cooked mustard oil or pure ghee.
34. **Kaddu raita**: Shredded and boiled pumpkin mixed with salted curd.
35. **Lesu:** Lesu is a local dish of Kumaon region, which is served for breakfast, lunch or dinner. This Kumouni bread is prepared by stuffing Madua dough into wheat flour dough. It is eaten with a lot of butter or ghee. It can also be served with curd and mixed pickle.
36. **Mixed Bhaddu Dal**: Bhaddu is a heavy bottom and narrow neck pot made of mix alloy.
37. **Pahari Rajma Daal**: A hilly species of Rajmas highly protein and delicious to eat
38. **Phaanu**: A dish like Chainsoo made of different variety of Daals like-Gahat, Arhar or green Mung and soaked in water for 4 to 5 hrs before cooked.
39. **Roat:** A mixture of wheat flour and sugar fried in oil
40. **Rus**: Kumaoni delicacy prepared with mixed dal stock, thickened by Rice paste and served with Rice.
41. **Sanaa hua chukh**: It is mouthwatering chutney from Kumaon, made from Pahadi lemon, radish, curd and spices.
42. **Sani Hui Mooli**: Slices of radish flavored with lemon, curd and paste of bhang seeds. Often used in winter.
43. **Sisaun or Sisunak Saag or Bicchu booti saag**: Tender leaves of —Bichhu Ghas‖ or nettle plant are picked for making the vegetable and it is tempered with Jakhya in mustard oil.
44. **Singal:** Singhal is a apiral traditional sweet festive snack from Kumaon, usually made for weddings and other occasions besides special festivals like Diwali and Holi. Made with mixture of semolina, yogurt and banana and then spiraled and deep fried.
45. **Siyal**: A sweet dish made from semolina and ripe bananas.
46. **Swala:** Spiced toor dal stuffed in wheat dough, flattened and deep fried.

47. **Thechwani:** Made by crushing of boiled potato or Radish
48. **Til ke Laddu:** Made of til and sugar
49. **Til ki Chutney:** Special in winter have tasty nature with Tor ki daal & Bhaat or with Gahat ke paranthe. Also used with various snacks items.
50. **Timur:** This is a hot pepper used in chutneys in northern part of Uttarakhand.
51. **Urad Dal ke Pakore** / Urad Bhuda: Spicy Pakoras made by mixture of different dal (Pulses)

CHAPTER TWENTY-SEVEN

Fairs and Festivals of Uttarakhand

Fairs and festivals for long have been the unique, interesting feature of the land of India and Uttarakhand is also no exception. In fact it won't be wrong to say that it's a land of fairs and festival. Uttarakhand, a land dotted with temples and more temples, has its own fairs and festivals, which are inherent to the culture here and have been passed from one generation to another since centuries. At such auspicious occasions, places of worship like Uttarakhand temples turn into venues of fairs and great celebration attracting people from far and wide. A fair held in the state is not just linked with its cultural identity but is also an important mark of its socio economic fabric. It offers glimpses of all aspects of a culture. A common trend in India and in Uttarakhand therefore is that many festivals come with their attached fairs.

1. **Jauljibi and Thal fair**: The fair of Jauljibi (or the Kumaoni festival as it is known) is held in the confluence of the rivers Kali and Gori of pithoragarh district every year in the month of November. It is also the place of meeting of three cultures- Shauka, Nepali and Kumaoni. Stressing on the significance of this place in the past and even today is the fact this is the getaway to important places like Johar, Darma, Chaudans and Byans. It was also once the centre point between Tibet and Tarai regions. While the fair is important for its commercial value yet its cultural significance is equally important. It invites visitors from as far as Nepal, who come here to sell horses, ghee and take back food grains and jaggary. A similar kind of fair is organized in Thal on the occasion of Makar Sankranti on the occasion of Vaishakh Sankranti on 14th April every year and is particularly famous with Shaukas.

2. **The Uttarayani Fair**: The Uttarayani fair is a very important fair to the cultural and social fabric of Uttarakhand. It is organized at not one but many places throughout the land of Uttarakhand- Bageshwar, Rameshwar, Suit Mahadev, Chitrashila (Ranibagh) and Hanseshwar. It is one of the oldest fairs of Kumaon also as the Makarsakranti or "sakrant" or 'Uttarayani Kauthik Mela' in local dialects. People from far-flung areas of Uttarakhand gathered here on the bank of Saryu and Gomti river to take a holy dip on the occasion of Sankrant or Makar Sankranti. It is believed that bathing on this day/festival is auspicious and it will wash away one's sins.
3. **Nanda Devi Fair**: Nanda Devi is the patron goddess of people of mountains. The Nanda Devi fair is held at many important cities across Uttarakhand like in Almora, Nainital, Kot, Ranikhet, Bhowali, Kichha and on a smaller level in villages of Lohar and in valleys of Pindar. According to the locals, the fair started in Kumaon region during the time of Kalyan Chand in 16th century. The fair is very important and sees visitors from far-flung areas. Rich with folk expression, the Nanda Devi fairs are also important from economical point of view.Famous Festivals of Uttarakhand.
4. **Gauchar Mela**: Gauchar Mela of Uttarakhand is a great attraction for the local people and the traders and merchants from every corner of the state. Held every year for a week starting from 14th November, Uttrakhand's Gaucher mela is fundamentally an industrial fair. It is attended widely by tourists and inhabitants of the state alike. The cultural programs like the local dances and songs always remains a major attraction of Gauchar mela at Uttarakhand.
5. **Peerane Kaliyar**: Peerane Kaliyar Festival is organised at Piran Kaliyar Sharif. This is located in Roorkee tehsil of Haridwar district. Lakhs of Jaireens from across the country and abroad participate in Peerane Kaliyar Festival. The festival spans for a period of about one month. It is organised on the basis of the Muslim calendar near Id-E-Milad.
6. **Ghughutia or Kale Kauva**: People make sweetmeats of flour and jaggery and make it in the shape of pomegranates, swords and knives and other such interesting shapes. A necklace is made with these then with an orange in the centre. Little children wear these and go out to attract crows and other birds and offer them pieces from their necklaces.
7. **Phool Dei**: The festival is celebrated in the beginning of month of Chaitra according to the Hindu calendar, which comes sometime in mid

March. It is mainly a festival of young girls, where in they go from house to house with plates full of rice, jaggery, coconut, green leaves and flowers. These girls give their blessings and wishes for the prosperity of the house and are given presents, jaggery, sweets, and money in return.

8. **Olgia or Ghiya sankranti**: The festival is celebrated on the first day of August or Bhado as it is called in the Hindi calendar. This is the time when the fields are full of lush green harvest and the milking animals are very productive. Earlier son in- laws to father and nephews to maternal uncles used to give presents, however now a days it has changed. People eat chapatis with ghee and urad dal (pulse) filled in it. Common presents that are exchanged include axes, ghee, *datkhocha* (metallic toothpick) and firewood. The festival's popularity has declined over a period of time.
9. **Khatarua**: While some say that the festival is celebrated in lieu of victory of king of Kumaon. But the popular belief goes that the festival marks the beginning of autumn season. It's celebrated sometime in mid September, the first day of month of Ashwin according to the Hindu calendar. Bonfires are lighted around which children dance. People offer cucumbers to fire as it is said to destroy all the evils. Special care is taken of animals during this time.
10. **Bat Savitri**: Another popular festival celebrated in entire northern India by married women for the well being of their spouses. The festival is celebrated on the last day of the dark half of the month of Jyeshtha according to Hindu calendar. Women worship Savitri who with her intense devotion brought her husband from death and observe fats. They also worship a holy tree called Bat or Banyan tree.
11. **Ganga Dusshera or Dasar**: The festival is celebrated sometime between May and June on the tenth day of the month of Jyeshtha according to Hindu calendar. This is the day of worshipping river Ganga and people take a dip in holy rivers. Many people put up stalls and offer water and food.
12. **Doonagiri mela**: Doonagiri mela Doonagiri, noted for its ancient Durga Temple, is a pilgrim spot that attracts a large of pilgrims, during the fair days at Navratri in October. Doonagiri Doonagiri is extremely rich in historical and religious significance and has many myths attached to it. According to one, when Hanuman was carrying the Sanjiwani booty to save Lakshman, a piece fell at this place and since that day, this place is known as Doonagiri. A temple of Vaishno Devi, the famous cave

Goddess, is situated here. Doonagiri is abuzz with activity in Chait and Ashwin months of Navaratris as many festivals are celebrated around that time.

13. **Kumaoni Holi**: The uniqueness of the Kumaoni Holi lies in its being a musical affair, whichever may be its form, be it the Baithki Holi, the Khari Holi or the Mahila Holi.The Baithki Holi and Khari Holi are unique in that the songs on which they are based have touch of melody, fun and spiritualism. These songs are essentially based on classical ragas. No wonder then the Baithki Holi is also known as Nirvan Ki Holi.The Baithki Holi begins from the premises of temples, where Holiyars (the professional singers of Holi songs) as also the people gather to sing songs to the accompaniment of classical music.Kumaonis are very particular about the time when the songs based on ragas should be sung. For instance, at noon the songs based on Peelu, Bhimpalasi and Sarang ragas are sung while evening is reserved for the songs based on the ragas like Kalyan, Shyamkalyan and Yaman etc. The Khari Holi is mostly celebrated in the rural areas of Kumaon. The songs of the Khari Holi are sung by the people, who sporting traditional white churidar payajama and kurta, dance in groups to the tune of ethnic musical instruments.
14. **Harela and Bhitauli**: On the first day of the navaratris (nine day holy period) of the month of Chaitra women fill baskets with soil and sow seven types of grains in them. The grains germinate symbolizing the future harvest. These yellow leaves, called Harela, are cut on the tenth day and people put them on their heads and behind their ears. During the month of Chaitra (March-April) brothers send presents to their sisters and parents to their daughters. These presents are called Bhitauli. However, the more popular Harela is the one that is celebrated in the month of Shravan to commemorate the wedding of Lord Shiva and Parvati and to welcome the rainy season and the new harvest. On this day people make Dikaras or clay statues of Gauri, Maheshwar, Ganesh etc. and worship them. Even the overworked bullocks are given a rest on the occasion of Harela. People put the blades of freshly cut Harela on their heads and send them to their relatives and friends as well.
15. **Kangdali**: Kangdali Festival is a celebrated by the Rung (Shauka) tribals of the Chaundas valley in Dharchula of the Pithoragarh District. It is held every twelve years between the months of August and October. It was last held in 2011. The festival coincides with the blossoming of the Kangdali plant, which flowers once every twelve years. According to

some accounts, Kangdali commemorates the defeat of Zorawar Singh's army, that had attacked this area from Ladakh in 1841. The Kangdali procession is a majestic march cum war-dance – armed with rills (a tool used in compacting the weave on the loom) the women lead the procession. The children and men armed with swords and shields follow compactly. As they sing and dance, their music echoes in the valley, and upon approaching the cursed shrubs (each village has a specific place where the shrubs are destroyed), music reaches its crescendo and the women begin the attack with their rills. The men follow and the bushes are hacked and uprooted and brought back, representing spoils of the war. More dance and song follows and the festivities culminate in a grand feast.

16. **Purnagiri Mela**: Purnagiri Mela is orgnised at Purnagiri Temple on the Annapoorna range during Chaitra Navratri in the month of March - Aprial . A large number of devotees visiting Purnagiri during this period. Although, devotees from all part of country visiting Purnagiri Temple throughout the year. The surrounding valleys echo with the holy chantings of the devotees climbing up to the top for darshan, creating an atmosphere of spirituality.
17. **Syalde Bikhauti Mela**: he Syalde – Bikhauti Mela is held in Syalde Pokhar in the old town of Dwarahat in Kumaon. It is an annual fair which is held every year in the month of Vaisakh (April/May). The fair commences with the beginning of the Hindu New year. The fair is held in two phases. The first one is held on the last day of the month of Chaitra at the Vimandeshwar temple of Lord Shiva, located eight kilometers from Dwarahat, while the other is held on the first day of Vaisakh at Dwarahat market. The preparations for the fair begin a month in advance in many surrounding villages. Singing of traditional Jhoda songs begins at the houses of the village chiefs.
18. **Hill Jatra**: Hilljatra is amongst the traditional festivals celebrated in the state of Uttarakhand, especially in Pithoragarh district of Kumaon Region. The festival is celebrated mainly by the people associated with farming in the state. Hill Jatra simply means the adoration (worshipping) of Hal (Plough) which good crop yield. It is essentially the festival of pastoralists and agriculturalists. The origin of this festival is believed to be from the Sorar Region of West Nepal to the Sor Valley and was initially introduced in Kumaour village. During the festival, a white-clothed deer is worshipped as a regional god. The festivity takes place in

three phase, and in the first phase sacrifice of goat is made with all the rituals, whereas in the second phase, dramas are performed for public and in the third and final phase, songs are sung and dance is performed.

19. **Tapkeshwar Mahadev Mela**: he cave temple dedicated to Shiva is situated at a distance of 6 kms from Dehradun and it turns into a huge fair site during the auspicious time of Maha Shivratri that generally falls during the months of Late February. Locally this fair is also referred to as _Shivratri Mela' and each year this place gets colored in various hues marking the marriage of Shiv and Parvati. People and devotees from various parts of the world make it a point to visit this temple at least once during this auspicious event.
20. **Bissu Mela**: The Jaunsari tribals of Uttarakhand celebrate a week long Bissu Fair marking the happiness and propersity coupled with the harvesting season. This fair is held in the Chakrata Block of Dehradun District. The Bissu Fair mirrors the plentiful cultural heritage and rich traditions of the Jaunsaris. People turn up in large numbers to participate in this fair from nearby Tehri, Uttarkashi and Saharanpur Districts. Bissu Fair is also celebrated at the well-known temple of Santoora Devi in close proximity to Kempty, about 5 kms from Mussoorie. The week-long fair is held during the Shukla Paksha in the month of Chaitra in accordance with the Hindu calendar.
21. **Egaas**: People of Uttarakhand Believe that Lord Rama returned from his exile 11 days late to the upper hilly regions. Which is why they celebrate Egaas, 11 days after Diwali by cooking various delicacies, lighting of candles and lamps, performing folk dances and lighting up their homes and people sing some local songs that are related specifically to Igaas Diwali.. People even celebrate by spinning a rope called "Bhailo" with a fire lit at one end.
22. **Basant Panchami**: Basant Panchami is the festival which celebrates the coming of Basant or Spring season. It is a significant festival in Uttarakhand. This festival marks the end of winter, a season of death and decay, and is celebrated in the month of Magh or January/ February. The locals dress themselves up in yellow clothing, perform Chounphula and Jhumelia dances and fly kites. They worship Saraswati, goddess of knowledge and prosperity and the land. Sweet rice is made in almost every home.
23. **Ramman**: Is a religious festival and ritual theatre of the Garhwal region in India. It is a festival of the Hindu community in celebrated in the

month of May or June in the twin town of the Saloor Dungra village of the Painkhanda Valley in the Chamoli district. It is celebrated in honour of the tutelary god, Bhumiyal Devta, a local divinity whose temple houses most of the festivities. This event is made up of highly complex rituals: the recitation of a version of the epic of Rama and various legends, and the performance of songs and masked dances. During this festival, Bhumiya Devta is taken by the local inhabitants in the form of a procession from his residing place to the central temple of the village. The procession is followed by beatings of drums and masked dance performances given by the locals.

24. **BagwalFair**: Bagwal Fair is celebrated at Maa Varahi Devi Temple in Devidhura located at a distance of 45 km from Lohaghat in the Champawat district of Uttarakhand on the occasion of Raksha Bandhan. Devidhura also marks the trijunction of Almora, Pithoragarh, and Nainital districts and is famous for its rich cultural heritage. Bagwal Fair is one such cultural fair that is celebrated with great zeal and devotion. It is a unique tradition in which two groups of devotees pelt stone at each other as part of a ritual named "Bagwal", while they try to protect themselves with the help of large wooden shields. Devotees flock to in large numbers to witness the festival.

CHAPTER TWENTY-EIGHT

Classical Recipes from the Uttarkhandi Kitchens

1. Aloo ke gutke

Ingredients:

- Potato -1Kg
- Cumin powder-½ Tsp
- Tumeric powder-1 Tsp
- Coriander powder-2 Tsp
- Red Chilli powder-1 Tsp
- Whole Red Chillies-5 gms
- Green Coriander-2 Bunches
- Oil-50 gms
- Salt- to taste

Method:

- Boil and peel the potatoes
- Cut the potatoes into small pieces
- Fry whole Red Chillies. (Keep it aside)
- Fry cumin seeds till it crakes then add tumeric powder
- Add boil potatoes pieces with Coriander powder and Salt.
- Cook on slow fire
- Garnish with chopped green Coriander and fried chillies.

2. Baadi

Ingredients:

- Kwada ka Aata -1-2 cup
- Water -as required
- Ghee -1-2 tbsp

Method:

- Heat water in a pan till it boils.
- Now mix Choon (kwada flour) in water and cook for 2 minutes.
- Add ghee to it and serve hot.

3. Chainsoo

Ingredients:

- Black Gram seeds(Kali Urd whole) -1 cup
- Oil -1/2 cup (preferably mustard oil)
- Garlic -4 to 5 cloves
- Cummin seeds -1 tsp
- Black pepper -4 nos.
- Red chillies whole -4 to 5
- Asafoetida -a pinch
- Dry coriander powder -1/2 tsp
- Turmeric powder -1/4 tsp
- Red chillies powder -1/2 tsp
- Water -3 cups
- Salt to taste
- Garam masala -1/2 tsp

Method:

- Place an iron frying pan (kadhai) on a moderate flame. Put Sabut Urad (black gram) in it and roast it without oil for about 3 to 5 minutes or till the pleasant aroma of roasted seeds comes. Do not over cook it. Take off the flame. Grind the roasted seeds into a coarse powder.

- Heat oil in the Kadahi and add garlic cloves.When the garlic turns lightl brown, add cumin seeds, red chillies,black pepper, and heeng (asafoetida)
- Immediately add the daal powder and fry it for 1-2 minute or so. Add turmeric powder, dry coriander powder, red chillies powder, salt and water. Bring it to boil.
- Cover and Cook till the daal becomes very soft. Simmer for 20-30 minutes. Before taking off the heat, sprinkle garam masala over chainsoo.
- Garnish with pure ghee and chopped coriander leaves.
- Serve with hot steamed rice.

4. Gahat (Kulath) ki Dal

Ingredients:

- Gahat (Kulath) -300 gms
- Tumeric -1 Tea Spoon
- Rice Paste -50 gms
- Coriander powder -1 Tea Spoon
- Red chilli powder -1 Tea Spoon
- Oil -50 ml
- Ginger -20gms
- Asafoetida Pinch
- Garlic -4-5 flakes
- Cumin Seeds -½ Tea Spoon
- Gandherin small piece

Method:

- Boil Gahat grain and add Ginger, Garlic,Tumeric,Coriander,Chilli powder and salt
- Add Rice paste and cook for sometime
- Temper with Cumin powder, Asafoetida and Gandharein.

5. Bhang ki Chutney

Ingredients:

- Bhang Seeds -50 gms
- Cumin Seeds -3 gms
- Lemon (Big) -One
- Salt to taste
- Whole Red Chillies -3 Pieces

Method:

- Roast Bhang seeds and cumin seeds separately
- Grind Red Chillies, Cumin seeds and Bhang seeds into fine paste adding little water.
- Squeeze Lemon juice into the paste, add salt and serve.

6. Jhangore ki Kheer

Ingredient:

- Jhangora -500 gms
- Sugar -200 gms
- Milk -2 Lts
- Cahewnuts -50 gms
- Raisins -50 gms
- Chironji -100 gms
- Kewara essence -2-3 drops.

Method:

- Wash and soak Jhangora in water for 1 hour.
- Boil Milk.
- Add Jhangora and stir well to avoid lumps.
- Add sugar and cook till it done.
- Add kewara essence and mix well.
- Garnish with Raisins, Cashewnuts, and Chironji.

CHAPTER TWENTY-NINE

Glossary: India's Himalayan Cuisine

1. Aktori - In Lahaul Spiti valley, the leaves of buckwheat are mixed with wheat flour and made into cakes.
2. Arsa - Fries dumplings made with sugar cane/ jaggary and rice. Served in pahadi wedding. (Uttarakhand)
3. Badi - Sun dried urad dal paste balls, used in Pahari vegetables and curries. (Uttarakhand)
4. Bhatt - Black pulse from Kumaun.
5. Bhuttua - Intestines, heart and liver of goat cooked together. (Uttarakhand)
6. Champaa - Roti made by Barley by the Bhutiyas.
7. Chhang - It is an indigenous rice beer made in the tribal belt of Lahaul & Spiti.
8. Chilla - KalanIt is the name given to 40 days of intense cold weather conditions in Jammu and Kashmir.
9. Czochworu - Is the desi donut which is a small, soft round bread of about three inches diameter and six inches circumference, with a soft upper half sprinkled with til (sesame seeds) or Khaskhash (poppy seeds) and the lower crust is crispy.
10. Dan - Is a three holed chullah used in Jammu and Kashmir.
11. Danda - Highly elevated land used for farming.(Uttarakhand)
12. Daru - local alcoholic beverage.(Uttarakhand)
13. Dhabadi - Arhar and palak dal from Garhwal.
14. Dubkas - Kumauni dal made from mung dal
15. Dubuk - Dal prepared with coarsly ground Bhatt or Gahat.(Uttarakhand)
16. Dulung - Special roti served to gods by the Bhotiyas.

17. Dum Aloo - Small poked potatoes are cooked in thin red gravy. (Kashmiri)
18. Gandreni - Aromatic root of plant used dals and curries. (Uttarakhand)
19. Gidkiyu - A soup made from Mandwa ata by the Bhotiyas. (Uttarakhand)
20. Jaama - Dried intestine of the wild goat, is also preserved by the Bhotiyas and used in many preparations during non- availablity of meat. (Uttarakhand)
21. Jadu - Jadu is like porridge. Prepared with I (buckwheat) flour, a Bhotiya speciality.
22. Jakhiya - Jakhiya is also known as wild mustard or dog mustard. It has sharp pungent smell and crunchy taste and so most Garhwalis prefer jakhiya over cumin and mustard seed for tempering.
23. Jambu - Wild herbs that are dried and used like we use kasuri methi. (Uttarakhand)
24. Jhol - Thin gravy
25. Jholi - Thick gravy made of pulses. (Uttarakhand)
26. Jhoom - Nomadic style farming.
27. Jya - Salted tea of Bhotiyas.
28. Kafal - Bay berries. Small berries of Kumaun region.2
29. Kedarkhand - Old name of Garhwal.
30. KehwaIs - green tea with spices and almonds. (Kashmir)
31. Khatta Maans - Is mutton cooked with sour pomegranate seeds (anardana) or lime juice and flavoured with fumes of a burning charcoal soaked in mustard oil.
32. Kodo Or Kodri - is a type of high mineral millet.
33. Kurunthi - Urad dal pakore. (Uttarakhand)
34. Kwacho - A kind of wild herb used in tempering. (Uttarakhand)
35. Lafhoo - Grated and sundried radish. (Uttarakhand)
36. Lengda - Wild asparagus. (Uttarakhand)
37. Lingadi - Fiddlehead fern, used as saag. (Uttarakhand)
38. Losar - Also known as Tibetan New Year. The festival is marked by worshipping the holy deity of the monastery to bring peace, happiness and good fortune for the incoming year.
39. Madra - Is a traditional spicy yogurt-based recipe. It can be cooked with chana, rajma, urad dal or raungi.
40. Madua - Finger millet. (Uttarakhand)
41. Manaskhand - Old name of Kumaun.

42. Mangodi - Dried dumpling mad from Moon dal, used inmaking curries. (Uttarakhand)
43. Marchhra - Chawlai seed. (Uttarakhand)
44. Marchu - These are fermented and deep-fried bread made of refined flour.
45. Mekauti - Kumauni name for malta.
46. Modhur Pulav - Sweetened Kashmiri rice prepared using cinnamon, a little saffron, milk, ghee, sugar, cashew nuts, almonds, green cardamom among several other ingredients.
47. Muji Gaad - It is a dish made up of fish prepared generally with radish or nadur. This dish is an amalgamation of vegetarian and non- vegetarian items as the taste of fish and lotus stem blend together to give it a unique taste while hot spices and herbs add to it's unique yet amazing flavour and aroma.
48. Nudu - Is a ceremonial food of Himachal Pradesh prepared by cooking wheat flour in milk with small amount of salt to be eaten with ghee.
49. Patende - It is a sort of pancake prepared from rice flour is popular in Hamirpur and Chamba districts.
50. Phanu - Dal made from gahat or kulath. (Uttarakhand)
51. Phasi - Wild goat in Uttarakhand
52. Quabargah - Ribs of young lamb or goat is cooked in a special blend of milk and spices, and then fried in ghee
53. Raintha - A traditional Himachali raita made with Khajur, Palak, and Walnut paste.
54. Rasialu - Himachali kitchen
55. Roat - Sweet Flatbread which is subtly flavoured with fennel seeds and cardamom. (Uttarakhand)
56. Rot - Is a dish made from dough of wheat flour and jaggery especially in the areas of Una, Hamirpur and Bilaspur.
57. Rotana - Sweet flour dumplings. (Uttarakhand)
58. Roth - Is a bulky bread laden with dry fruits and coconut with a sweet tinge.
59. Rus - A delicacy made from mixed dal stock thickened with rice flour. (Uttarakhand)
60. Samovar - This is a jug-shaped metallic pitcher used for brewing tea such as *Kehwa* and *Sheer chai*. It has a long tube inside that is filled with charcoal, which keeps the tea in the pot brewing.

61. Sancholoo - Is another popular sweet dish from Hamirpur made from wheat flour, ghee and grated coconut.
62. Sheermal - Is a sweet bread prepared using refined flour, milk, saffron and dates and has its own flavor. It's like a delicious biscuit. Crisp, crumbly and flavorful.
63. Shufta - Shufta is Kashmiri dessert that is made up of a lot of dry fruits and sugar.
64. Singal - Fried spirals of Samolina / Rice Flour, a sweet delicacy. (Uttarakhand)
65. Sisunag - Nettle leaves. (Uttarakhand)
66. Siyal - Sweet dish made from semolina and ripe bananas. (Uttarakhand)
67. Surka - A local beverage made from fermented wheat. (Uttarakhand)
68. Swala - Spiced toor dal stuffed in wheat dough, flattened and deep fried. (Uttarakhand)
69. Thawe - Nigella seeds.
70. Thechwani - Dish made by crushing of boiled potato or Radish. (Uttarakhand)
71. Thenthuk - A noodle soup prepared with wheat flour dough, mixed vegetables, and some pieces of mutton or Yak meat are added to enhance its taste and value.
72. Thukpa - Rice or vegetable stew from the Bhotiyas.
73. Timur - This is a hot pepper used in chutneys.
74. Toda - It is made from maize or bajra flour or rice flour. Flour is wetted with warm water and is constantly rubbed with the palm. It is then rounded, flattened and baked on tawa.
75. Tsoek - Kidney or liver of lamb cooked delicately with assorted spices
76. Ver - Is a secret spice mixture used in foods to give them a Kashmiri flavour. It contain garlic and praan for Muslims, asafoetida and fenugreek for Hindus as well as lots of freshly ground red chillies, cumin, coriander, dried ginger, cloves, cardamom and turmeric.
77. Wazas - Are professional Kashmiri cooks.
78. Wazwan - It is the name of Kashmiri Muslim banquet.

CHAPTER THIRTY

Summary: History of India's Himalayan Cuisine

Cuisine of Jammu and Kashmir has become world famous for its uniqueness and variety. The most famous Kashmiri non-veg dishes named Wazwan are seekh kababs, tabak maz Roganjosh, Yakhni and Gushtaba, and the renowned veg dishes are Dum Aloo and Chaman. The cuisine is now compared to other international cuisine's like Continental cuisine, Chinese cuisine and Indian cuisine. Cuisine of Jammu and Kashmir is nothing less than a treasure for the food lovers. The cuisine here is absolutely different from the cuisine of north India. In fact, every region has its own specialty. Unlike in other parts of India, the meals here are highly dominated by non- vegetarian dishes and the staple food here is rice. The variety during festivals is simply unimaginable and this variety brings a new edge to your travel in J&K during festivals. One thing you will never remember about your meal is the number of dishes you had as you will be served with endless amount of courses. The use of spices in every dish is also highly intriguing in Kashmiri food.

Non Vegetarian Delicacies: In Jammu and Kashmir, the one thing that everyone has almost every second day is non-vegetarian food. The grand feast, the 36-course meal that is called Wazwan, has around 30 non-veg dishes. The people who cook these gigantic feasts are called 'Wazas', the descendants of great chefs who were the masters of the unique art of cooking. The experimentation with the food that they do, is simply astounding. Almost every dish has a variant that is as good as the original, if not better. The main item that is served is rista (meatballs). They are made by finely smashing mutton and cooking it in gravy. In fried variety, you will find seekh kababs, tabak maz which are fried till the time they get a very crunchy and crispy texture. Other famous and mouth watering non veg dishes that are served in the Wazwan are Roganjosh, Yakhni and Gushtaba. The cuisine in the Ladakh area has a strong resemblance to the cuisine in Tibet and the cooking style is also very similar. The Ladakhis prefer to eat rice, wheat, millet, yak butter, and other dairy products along with vegetables and fruits.

Vegetarian Cuisine: Although you will not find many vegetarian dishes here, but few that are there are exquisitely delicious. The most famous veg dish of all is Dum Aloo (steam cooked potato curry) and Chaman (cheese) that have made a mark not only in Jammu and Kashmir but in entire country. Few years back, a pure vegetarian had to struggle a lot to find a suitable place where he can get vegetarian food. But now, keeping its tradition of warm hospitality, the state has opened up many restaurants that cater to their vegetarian guests and take good care of them.

After such a sumptuous meal, one really does not have any space left in stomach, but try making a bit as the special sweet dish is still remaining. Fireen is the name of that special dish that will keep your taste buds happy till the time you remember this dish. You can also enjoy the local snacks like Sheermal and baqerkhani, tsot and tsochvoru are different form of Kashmiri breads. All this only adds to the already vast range of delicacies in the Jammu and Kashmir cuisine.

> *"So much variety, so many flavors, such taste, you will get all this only in the cuisine of Jammu and Kashmir. The tremendous options and variety of food is seldom seen any place else. There are many hotels and restaurants that offer you the best of dishes from Kashmir."*

The Cuisine of Himachal Pradesh - the north Indian state lying at the foothills of the Himalayas - boasts of a uniqueness of its own. Influence of the neighboring lands of Punjab and Tibet is clearly evident in the Himachal cuisine. Besides, the geographical and climatic conditions of the state have a strong effect on the dishes of Himachal Pradesh and the way they are prepared. The day-to-day cuisine of Himachal Pradesh is simple and very much similar to that of other north Indian states. Rice, paddy and maize constitute the staple diet of the people here. But the preferred taste varies from region to region. Thus, while in the barren regions of Kinnaur and Lahaul-Spiti, locally-grown coarse grains like buckwheat, millet and barley are mainly used, regions with pastoral tradition use large quantities of milk and its products in their dishes.

Non-vegetarian food, with liberal usage of spices like cardamom, cinnamon, cloves and red chilies, form an integral part of the cuisine of Himachal Pradesh. The local people are not known to be particularly fond of vegetarian fare. In the average Himachal households, all kinds of meat, lentil and cereal preparations are generally cooked.

A typical everyday meal in the cuisine of Himachal Pradesh comprises 'dal-chawal-subzi- roti' (the common north Indian fare of lentil broth, rice, vegetable curry and bread). Special dishes are cooked during festive occasions. Some of the popular dishes in the cuisine of Himachal Pradesh include 'Sidu' - a kind of bread made from wheat flour. It is generally eaten with ghee (clarified butter), dal or mutton. Among the festival dishes prepared in Himachal Pradesh, 'Dham' - atraditional festive meal is the most popular one. This dish is cooked by only a particular caste of Brahmins called 'botis'. Preparations for this elaborate mid-day meal start the night before. Dham is served in courses on epattalsi or leaf plates. 'Ankolas' made of rice flour are also famous festive dishes in many parts of the state. In drier areas like Lahaul-Spiti valley, the leaves of buckwheat are mixed with wheat flour and made into cakes called 'aktori'. 'Patande' - a kind of pancake is a famous specialty in the Sirmaur area.

The cuisine of Uttarakhand: Snuggled in the foot hills of the majestic Himalayas, Kumaon and Garhwal are two distinct constituent regions. Both have their own distinctive traditions, festivals and culture and their Cuisine is high on taste and nutrition. The food habits of the people change according to the changing seasons.

> "*The cuisine of Uttarakhand, to say the least, unconventional is strongly influenced by the geography of Uttarakhand. Which are the main ingredients used in the cuisine found in and around the mountains, forests and lakes of Uttarakhand with a number of vegetables, pulses and cereals availability which are rarely found in other parts of the world.*"

Where great care is taken to include all the necessary elements to keep one well- prepared for the tough climate and trails, special attention is paid to maintaining the look and taste of the dishes as well. A balanced flavour is the key to authentic Uttarakhand cuisine that is mostly cooked over slow fire and consists of lentils. Although Kumaon and Garhwal are divided in different regions; they unite as one in its methods of cooking and the choice of ingredients. There are also several dishes that two regions are common but have different names. The food habit in the state also witness variation with the changing season; where in winter in Mathir and Til Laddus or Madua Rotis are preferred, in summers, Dubkas with Chholia Rotis are relished.

The major ingredients responsible for adding the taste and incredible aroma to the food of Uttarakhand are varied lentils that are exclusive to the state and variety of flours that come from barley and buck wheat. The dishes in Garhwal deeply connects to its people, the food is prepared with the right amount of spices, which only entices one to savour it. Phanu, Kafuli, Thechwani, Chainsoo, Jholi, Gahat ke Paranthe, Roat and Baadi are some of finger-licking Garhwali dishes. Meanwhile in Kumaon, Aaloo ke Gutke, Dubke, Thathwani, Kaapa, Chudkani, Jaula,Kandalee ka Saag and Sisunaak Saag are the mouth-watering presentations. Owing to milk abundance the locals of Garhwal are very fond of dairy product. The side dishes in Uttarakhand are equally important and therefore are prepared with utter care, Bhangeera ki Chutney, Mooli Thechuwa and Hara Namak are some of the sides that add to the flavour of main course meals. Concluding the gastronomic journey in Uttarakhand are its melt in mouth deserts, of which Singal-Puha, Jhangora ki Kheer, Singodi and Baal Mithai are few prelude. One noticeable and worthy of trial is "Sanaa Hua Nimbu", which is by far the clear attention grabber in the palatable cuisine of Uttarakhand. **People of this state are meticulous, honest and courageous as we know about it.**

Know Your Author

Dr Anshumali Pandey, PhD, Author

Dr. Anshumali Pandey, is a renowned & reliable name in the field of Education, Hospitality, Tourism and Tribal Food. He is a Teacher and Chef by profession, and also an Author, a Business Auditor, and an avid culinary traveller to the Indian Sub continental hinterlands. Dr. Anshumali Pandey is a Hospitality Educator (PhD) who specialises in Higher Education, Office Administration, Pay roll, HR, Labour Laws, Audit, and Procurement & Tender Process. He is an Author with 52 Publications consisting of 37 Books.

The books written by **Dr Anshumali Pandey** are essentially a banquet arising from an experience of over 25 years of Professional life and have boiled down to crisp and accurate writing on his favourite subjects. Hospitality Sector champion requires to be a specialist in many fields and Dr Pandey is one of them. His knowledge is evident from the spectrum of subjects which he has chosen for his books so far, which ranges from being a specialist chef, to Master of Human resources, to Education and to love for children, and topped with Spirituality.

Books written by the Author are –

1. Theory of Indian Cookery
2. Beauty and Irony of Silvassa Tourism
3. A Short Indian Food Story
4. Be Your Own Guide to Indian Cuisine
5. Cookery Fundamentals
6. History of Indian Food (2 Editions Printed)
7. The Great Indian Story Book for Children
8. Personal Budget: Easy Work Book
9. Online Classes Log Book
10. Dictionary Making Work Book for School Children
11. The Lazy Bed
12. Hindu Dharm (हिन्दू धर्म) (In Hindi Language)
13. Where is my coffee?
14. Your First Job is Never your Last (Volume 1)
15. You are Almost There (Quick Fix Resume and Interview Hacks)
16. Working for the Enemy? - A lesson in Career Management
17. Public Speaking for the Young
18. A Date With Coffee
19. How to be The Best Hotel Front Office Employee
20. Diploma in Food Production, The complete Syllabus
21. Diploma in F&B Service, The Complete Syllabus
22. Diploma in Front Office, The Complete Syllabus
23. The Time to Speak is Now
24. Munshi Premchand (Short Stories in English)
25. The Housekeeping Department, Text Book
26. Hitchhiker's Guide to Trekking in Uttarakhand
27. Uttarakhand, A divine Land for a Reason
28. Bachhon ke liye rochak kahaniyan (बच्चों के लिए रोचक कहानियाँ) (In Hindi Language)
29. Basic Communication Skills of English
30. The Basic Office Organisation Book for Start-ups
31. Hospitality HRM
32. Hospitality Marketing
33. Bakery Ingredients and Tools

34. Human Resource Management for Indian Professionals
35. The process of LAWFULLY operating a Hospitality business in India
36. Indian Classical Sweets: History, Tradition and Recipes
37. History of India's Himalayan Cuisine: Classical Cookery of Kashmir, Laddakh, Jammu, Himachal, Lahaul, Spiti, Garhwal, Kumaon.

Connect with me: anshumali.pandey@gmail.com
https://notionpress.com/author/337004

Author's Qr Code:

Please Scan the above QR Code with your Smart Phone to get online information about the Author and his Books.

www.ingramcontent.com/pod-product-compliance
Lightning Source LLC
LaVergne TN
LVHW020119090726
842905LV00041B/1093